O U T

O F

A CELEBRATION OF CONTEMPORARY BOX ART
TOM BUCHANAN

T H E

B O X

eightbooks

8

eightbooks

First published in 2022 by
Eight Books Ltd
40 Herbert Gardens
London NW10 3BU

info@8books.co.uk
www.8books.co.uk

A catalogue record for this book is available
from the British Library.

ISBN 978 1 9998583 8 4

Graphic design by Transmission
www.transmission.design

Additional photography by Peter Mallet

Editing and proofreading by Mark Ralph

Printed and bound in Latvia by Livonia

Front cover
CHICK
by Nancy Fouts
2012, 12 × 10 × 10 cm
Taxidermy chick in glass bell jar
www.nancyfouts.uk

Back cover
MADONNA & CHILD
by Peter Quinnell
2012, 26 × 15 × 12 cm
Mixed-media assemblage

Endpapers
Front: BOXED UP *by Maha Ahmed*
Back: DICE *by Martin O'Neill*

Opposite
IBM 2401, 1964
by Docubyte

Pages 4-5
NEON SIGN
by Tom Buchanan and Philip Oakley
2012, 33 × 244 × 20 cm
Glass tubing, electronics, recycled wood

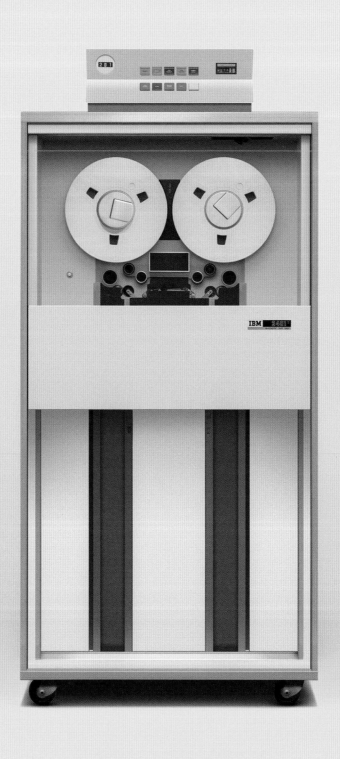

THE BOX

OUT OF THE BOX

BOX [BOKS]

To describe non-conformist, novel, or creative thinking. Some innovative way or breakthrough.

"Out of the box, mate!" (Australian slang): remarkable or exceptional; extraordinary.

To think out of the box (or thinking beyond the box) is a metaphor for thinking differently, unconventionally, or from a new perspective.

To explore ideas that are original and unusual and that are not limited or controlled by rules or tradition.

Speculating beyond its restrictive confines, the metaphorical "box" in the phrase can be both (a) positive, fostering creative leaps, as in generating wild ideas (the conventional use of the term); and (b) negative, penetrating through to the "bottom of the box."

A frank and insightful re-appraisal of a situation or oneself.

Adjective

Crazy, irrational. Note: it has been theorized that the term is a vague allusion to the jack-in-the-box toy, a box containing a bouncing head mounted on a spring that pops open after a crank has been turned. The unpredictable motion of the head could be likened to someone who is "out of the box."

Any sensible person will tell you that s/he prefers an out-of-the-box solution.

It has become something of a cliché, especially in the business world, where "thinking outside the box" has become so hackneyed as to be almost meaningless.

Noun

A container, case, or receptacle, usually rectangular, of wood, metal, cardboard, etc., often with a lid or removable cover.

"Be a box of birds" is to be happy or in good health.

A difficult situation or predicament.

A small enclosure or area in a courtroom, for witnesses or the jury.

(Chiefly British) A gift or present; "a Christmas box." Customarily given to tradesmen as thanks for good service throughout the year.

Slang

An attractive female; a Police interrogation room; a coffin.

THE SECOND STATE
by Daniel Agdag
2018, 58 × 30.5 × 30.5 cm
Cardboard, tracing paper,
timber base

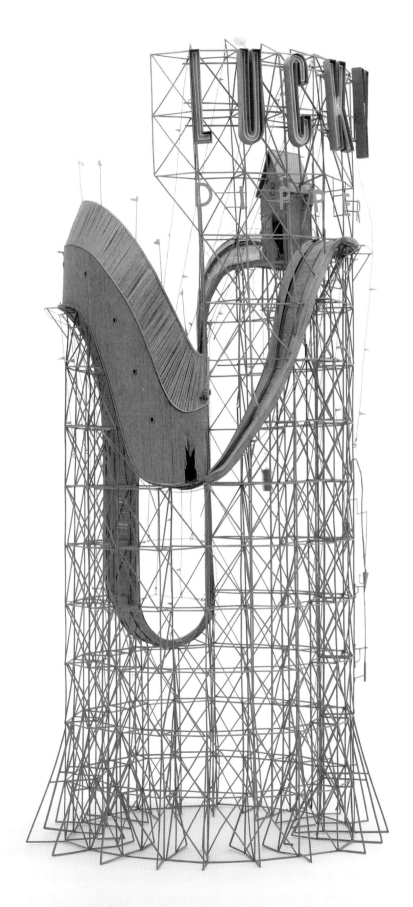

C O

E N

PREFACE

TOM BUCHANAN

"THE BOXES CALLED THE WRITERS FROM GREAT DISTANCES; THEY DEMANDED THE ATTENTION OF THOSE WHO HAD NO ATTENTION TO SPARE"

A CONVERGENCE OF BIRDS
ORIGINAL FICTION AND POETRY INSPIRED BY THE WORK OF JOSEPH CORNELL, EDITED BY JONATHAN SAFRAN FOER

There is an ingenuous, primal-stomper of a song called "Little Room" by Jack White of the White Stripes. In essence, it is a story about a modest place in which you start making something rather special, which inevitably leads to needing an even bigger place to work; but once you actually get there, you might have to question how you ever started out. I am tickled by the urgency of the lyrics, which could speak volumes for the authenticity of any creative endeavour. But for me, the little room in question could easily be one of my box works—the impulse to capture or contain some kind of magic before it has any chance of escaping. That thrill of closing the lid, setting the trap, and tiptoeing away can be a bold revelatory feat, as urgent as putting a message into a bottle and throwing it out to sea. I like to think of box art as a time capsule, a chamber of secrets.

BEGINNINGS

The first micro-worlds I ever made were probably action scenes or dioramas, formed in old shoe boxes or containers for my army and Star Wars figures. Through these little portals I could go anywhere; it was up to me, free-wheeling in my own storytelling. I come from the "Why don't you just switch off your television set and go and do something less boring instead?" generation, when an old cereal packet, a used bottle of washing-up liquid, and a tub of PVA glue would go a long way. Such self-belief could quickly result in an epic sci-fi shadow-puppet show at the top of the stairs, using a torch against a screen of baking paper, while ELO blasted out on cassette. It did not matter that the audience was just cuddly toys and a startled babysitter. On my sixth birthday, my mum asked me what kind of decoration I would like on my birthday cake, to which I apparently replied, "Dead soldiers." There is no visual proof to share, but she covered that cake in a blizzard of white marzipan, divided down the middle by a plastic barbed-wire fence. Two of my toy soldiers had been clipped at the base and laid stiff on either side of the fence, like a scene from the Battle of Stalingrad. I was too young to remember my friends' faces when the cake was rolled out at my party, but I sure was punch-proud. This proved an informative lesson in perversity for a worthy cause. Like a toy box, arranging such worlds brings out our childlike instincts, a time when we had the most freedom to try things out.

> "Collecting is a kind of poetry: it's a shuffling around of objects and spaces until they make sense."
> Edmund de Waal, ceramicist and author

I have always enjoyed taking the familiar towards the unfamiliar. The act of placing things into unlikely relationships with other objects can help us pursue a whole different train of thought. I have worked as a graphic artist for twenty-five years across all aspects of design. Bewitched by early memories of Ray Harryhausen, penny arcade automata, and London's Pollock's Toy Museum, I have long been fascinated by such original masters of illusion as Georges Méliès and Jan Švankmajer. They could transport you to fantastical realms you could almost grasp and touch. This enduring love for the tactile led to an exploratory journey into dimensional illustration, unconventional scenarios made up of textures, original imagery, and found objects. In effect, I was forming an animated freeze, layered together like a suspended stage set. The discovery of this extended frame provided a space that is public yet private, capturing moments in time that seem intimate yet somehow universal. Working simultaneously as an artist, I have also done much gardening and landscaping over the years, sourcing endless material from the soil and undergrowth, characterfully unique in its preserved state of decay. These magpie moments are mystical—I am the chosen one, unearthing treasure ordained for some higher purpose, just like receiving that message in a bottle washed up on the shore.

CABINETS OF CURIOSITY

In the madness of the Covid-19 pandemic, it was strangely diverting to know that the first man to receive the Pfizer-BioNTech vaccine was called William Shakespeare (reflecting, perhaps, the fact that the original Shakespeare's life was also marked by plague). This absurd newsflash made me think of a time capsule, of how the contents within might just bamboozle the universe. Just imagine a distant planet discovering a medieval suit of armour, along with a stuffed dodo and a can of baked beans, all conserved in a dusty rocket. What would these assorted trophies tell some passing intergalactic explorer about our planet? Maybe a box can help us let go, or allow us to question the very interior of things.

A vitrine or glass cabinet was originally adopted by the Church as a way of preserving or glorifying the relics of saints. The display of the most humble object could be singularly transformed into something hallowed and holy. A perfect present-day testament to this process is musician Warren Ellis's essential memoir *Nina Simone's Gum*. In 1999, Dr Nina Simone gave one of her final UK performances in front of a spellbound Ellis (and a few other fans), who, in transcendental awe, scrambled onto the stage after the show, took the piece of chewed gum stuck to the singer's piano, and wrapped it in her stage towel, which he then stuffed into a Tower Records bag. The gum remained safely stashed away for twenty years until Ellis's collaborator Nick Cave offered his friend the chance to place the gum on a marble plinth. Housed in a glass case, the mounted gum is now on show at the Royal Danish Library for all to see.

In Renaissance Europe, cabinets of curiosities, otherwise known as *Wunderkammer*, were regarded as a microcosm, a memory theatre of the world. These early museum–like wonder-rooms were filled with collections of encyclopedic objects and oddities whose categorical boundaries were yet to be defined. Some say they were a form of propaganda, often filled with faked remnants, symbolizing in miniature the control of the powerful over the powerless. Wealthy rulers, collectors, and merchants had the ability and resources to stir our sense of bewilderment, leaving us to marvel at the fact that the world might be flat and the oceans full of mermaids. But why should we trust everything we see? Presentation can be so seductive that we are constantly cajoled into believing.

As a rule, creatives tend to be voracious collectors. Seeking, locating, acquiring, classifying, cataloguing, storing, and displaying are all vital practices to aid the artistic soul. However demented these activities might appear to others, they provide some kind of ordered path through the everyday. Like a souvenir, it is instinctive to preserve and protect the contents of such collections, whatever they might be—an act of remembrance that can determine how we inhabit the present. The English rock star Phil Collins collects artefacts related to the Battle of the Alamo. In 2014, Collins donated his private collection of such artefacts—the largest-known of its kind—to the Texas General Land Office, guardian of the Alamo, earning him the title of "true Texan." It is amazing to think that a boy from London, inspired by the 1950s Disney television series *Davey Crockett*, would one day spend his time and money collecting rare cannon balls from the Lone Star state.

OUT OF THE BOX

"Artworks which have evolved, been created within, or even escaped from a box." This was how I worded my 2012 nationwide open invitation, an experimental call-out to a debut show entitled *Out of the Box*. The remarkable response it received turned a personal interest into the curating and subsequent writing of this book. Never could I have anticipated such an enthusiastic reaction from so many walks of life. The "Roll up! Roll up!" nature of the exhibition gave its title new purpose. Contributors came in all shapes and sizes, from professional practitioners to genuine outsider artists, all heading in different directions, deconstructing and re-assembling, making the concept their very own. The first event, at Brighton Festival, introduced me to such vital personalities as Peter Quinnell, Stephen Wright, and Maria Rivans, to name but a few. The call-out encouraged diversity by way of practice, restoring a forgotten "wow" in the things around us and providing a unique platform from which to reframe the commonplace. Through kinship and chance encounter, *Out of the Box* was invited to arts events and festivals across the UK, including Fringe Arts Bath, Danny Boyle's Shuffle Festival, and a residency at London's No Format Gallery.

As curator, I could witness the engagement of the general public first-hand, people of all ages responding to the versatility and scope of the work, beyond any expectations of an art experience. Is it fine art or crafts? To me, box art is neither a genre nor a medium. There is, however, a definite tangible thrill, triggering a nostalgia-infused antidote to these hyperbolic, multimedia times. Conversations among visitors to the shows ranged from forgotten toys, grandma's button sets, and how best to arrange a larder to the merits of mudlarking on the shores of the River Thames. The exhibitions also seemed to resonate with such contemporary concerns as the impulse to hoard and our need to upcycle. Interestingly, archaeologists use "grave goods"—things our early ancestors placed with the dead—as indicators of cultural intelligence. What gives these imperfect objects, these fluke artefacts, their value is that they tell the stories of our lives; they have a history just like us, resonant with memory. I am sure that, in lockdown, we have all found some kind of solace or salvation in our attics and cupboards—whether real or of the mind—rediscovering hobbies that can be worked in miniature.

"Finding similarities in things that are different
and finding differences in things that are similar."
Bill Hicks, comedian and satirist

There is a vitality to the spontaneous nature of box art, which is as amusing as it is addictive. My initial interest in the subject soon turned into a global investigation and the discovery of such diverse and far-flung work as the fables of Hari & Deepti from Mumbai, Kim Bumsu's South Korean cinefilm shrines, and Mohamad Hafez's reflections from Syria. As an artist, this journey has proved a life-affirming exchange, making palpable connections with such different worlds. Box art touches every aspect of our lives, not least our tendency to rationalize and organize, making it extremely accessible. We live, arrange, watch, and even die in boxes, which somehow helps us relate to the absurdity of life. In presenting the wild spirit of this practice, I have chosen to celebrate the artists through the universal truths of the four elements, in all their erratically sublime manifestations. Like the logic in hanging these artworks within a space, stories unfurl as inevitably as the destructive passion of fire, the permanence of earth, the perceptive travels of air, and the introspective calm of water.

I decided that the opening chapter should be "Water," beginning with a series of origin stories, histories that go back to the source, questioning where things come from and our long-standing relationship to objects. Water is also symbolic of fertility and reflection, opening up more reflexive notions of the box, such as its functionality or as a tool for healing. The flow of this first chapter leads naturally into "Earth," influenced by nature and organic form. "Earth" is also very much about creativity, with an emphasis on home, shelter, and stability. Next comes the most masculine of the chapters, "Fire," demonstrating lust, power, assertiveness, and renewal. Finally, we have "Air," the most conceptual instalment of the book, sharing innovation, communication, and perception, as well as travel, harmoniously taking

the journey full circle. Each chapter features a number of photographic stories. Not only are these works of art in their own right, but also they make a veritable case for the function or necessity of a box, in the significance of the stories they tell. Like all the artists, the subjects of these stories are collectors too, archiving their own personal typologies of what makes us who we are. Such anthropological quests to understand ourselves are also celebrations of fading art forms, inviting us to places we might never see. As a Londoner, many of these encounters have somehow brought me closer to nature, as did the very place where this venture began: the magical hub that is Hastings, on the south coast of England.

PORTALS

I was once asked to describe what box art means to me in a single word. Without thinking, I blurted out "freedom"—a wry quip, suggesting entrapment or possibly even a life sentence. I think I was trying to convey the idea that a box provides me with a place to reveal my better self. But the honesty of that exchange reminded me of a story by the late American writer Barry Lopez called "Emory Bear Hands' Birds." An imprisoned Native American known as Emory inspires his fellow inmates with stories and folklore about the wisdom of animals, about how each of us has a totem guardian that can take care of us. Stuck inside a Californian federal prison among some of the most dangerous offenders in the country, Emory's audience find some kind of hope and purpose in his stories. He urges them to keep council with their totem spirits so that, one day, they can all turn into birds and fly away.

Directly inspired by an avian-themed box work by Joseph Cornell—arguably the godfather of box art—Lopez's story was one of twenty-two featured in *A Convergence of Birds*, a collection of experimental fiction and poetry similarly inspired by Cornell's artwork. On a whim, Jonathan Safran Foer, then an unpublished college student, sent some prints of Cornell's works to a selection of his favourite authors, asking each of them to respond to the prints with a piece of writing. This astounding anthology was given to me as a present at one of the first *Out of the Box* exhibitions. It was the perfect companion piece, the contributors being so eclectic and endlessly imaginative.

In 2015, an extraordinary retrospective of Cornell's work was held at the Royal Academy of Art in London. Entitled *Wanderlust*, the exhibition's theme was Cornell's obsession with travel. A man who rarely left his home in the New York borough of Queens, let alone crossed the ocean, filled his art with mementoes of places that he had visited only in his imagination. Even his address was slightly unreal: 3708 Utopia Parkway. Cornell made boxes to keep wonders in. Full of intricate magic, poetry, and secrets, they were created in the basement beneath the small wooden house that he shared with his mother and disabled younger brother, whom he cared for. Cornell did not need to travel because his wanderlust was satisfied by his own private voyages and flights of the mind. His paradise could be found in the ephemera of the streets, junk shops, book stalls, and newspaper stands of the city.

Box art is constantly alive with the possibility of discovery and re-inventing the ordinary. To borrow a phrase from Frank Jennings, a friend and one of the artists featured in this book, creators of box art are makers of "deceptive receptacles"—small discoveries that can both surprise and take us places.

BOX ART
AN ART-HISTORICAL CONTEXT
SARAH LEA

In 2014 I visited the No Format Gallery in London to see *Out of the Box*, curated by Tom Buchanan. I was in the midst of researching another exhibition: *Joseph Cornell: Wanderlust* (Royal Academy of Arts, 4 July–27 September 2015). Meeting Tom and talking with him about the artists he knew confirmed that Cornell, an American artist who created his first shadow boxes in the early 1930s and died in 1972, continued to provide inspiration to many artists in London, despite his work being under-represented in UK public collections. Most knew Cornell's art only via photographs and books, just as reproductions of places and things Cornell had never seen sustained his own itinerant imagination: his body never strayed far from New York City, but the works he made—like his mind—ranged far and wide.

My first encounter with his art took place in Venice. I was sixteen, standing at the mantelpiece inside the unfinished eighteenth-century Palazzo Venier dei Leoni (converted into the home of Peggy Guggenheim and her collection from 1949). There were four boxes: a fortune-telling parrot, a flight over the Swiss Alps to the tune of cow bells, a palace within a palace, and an apothecary fit for an alchemist. They felt immediately familiar, and yet wondrous—an invitation to join the travels of the artist in these "cabins of the mind."

The shadow box—a glass-fronted, usually wooden cabinet—is a very particular structure: it has the independence of a sculpture; it has a frame that brings with it the perspectival pull of the Western tradition of painting; and, through the inclusion of found objects and photographs, it has an indexical relationship to the world common to collage and assemblage. In this hybrid, liminal place, things begin to behave like images, and images have the power of the real. A precise yet insistently provisional relationship between textures and pictorial elements is possible. The operation of montage—that magic moment when two or more images collide and create something new—are in a perpetual state of occurrence. In some instances, implied possibilities become actually dynamic: the work might have moving parts, or be opened so that components might be handled and re-arranged. In this way, sound and duration are activated, enriching this already rich spatial, visual, tactile, and temporal medium.

Perhaps it is through these multisensory dimensions that box art sails so close to the winds of our everyday experience: day-to-day stuff and ordinary cognitive reactions are reconfigured. Our perceptions and memories are set in motion. In the prolific, labyrinthine written musings that manifest Cornell's practice of "diarying," he reflects on the "warp and woof of daily life" and arrives at the deceptively simple equation: "collage = *life*." But this really is how our brains understand the world, by archiving references that influence our reactions to new stimuli. The box contains the fragments, and our minds work outwards from there, remembering, making sense, imagining, dreaming . . .

This form has been taken up by different groups of artists, often as a means of escaping the boundaries of the gallery or transgressing the conventions of the "rational" museum (and its predecessor, the *Wunderkammer*). From Dada and its surrealist affiliates in the 1920s and 1930s, to their conceptual-art corollaries of the 1960s and 1970s such as Fluxus, to more recent artists including Mark Dion, the box has proved an important tool in critiquing the functions of institutional collecting. Yet in recent years a shift has happened, a gathering recognition of the crucial role of collecting as a driving force for a range of artistic practices; for example, overtly in the powerful assemblage work of Betye Saar, and in the background for such artists as Tacita Dean. What counts here is not the categorization of objects according to museological systems, but their totemic qualities. The activity of collecting is a fundamental instrument of creativity in general, and poetic association in particular, a notion captured by Cornell's terminology: his "sketchboxes" would be filled with loosely related materials, waiting for a moment of coalescence.

Despite Cornell having admirers among leading twentieth-century collectors, museums, and artists (he was in creative dialogues with several such individuals, ranging from Marcel Duchamp, maker of the famous *La Boîte-en-Valise* ("Box in a Suitcase," 1935–41), to Yayoi Kusama, who creates boxes into which we can step), he was not convinced that his works belonged "within the category of art" at all. With no formal artistic training, he insisted he was only a "maker" operating in a "Sunday spirit," with works often "sparked" by an encounter with a new find, deepened by his autodidactic research into such specialist subjects as early cinema and ancient astronomy.

This is another of the special qualities that box art possesses: it is a paradigm with an affinity for the amateur—in the sense of a practice undertaken for the love of it—reflecting the French origin of the phrase. Historical precedents abound outside the confines of the modernist art canon: the découpage or shell-work shadow boxes of the domestic Victorian era, the hobbyist mounting collections of specimens, the miniature childhood worlds of dolls houses and train sets. The box also recalls technologies of display stretching back into history: the television, the aquarium, the puppet theatre, the camera obscura . . .

The first box? Pandora's, perhaps?

Thornton Dial's *The Art of Alabama* is a monument to the assemblage works and traditions of the African American yard show, which reclaimed art for communities not represented in the canon and museums of Western art history. The sculpture, made in 2004, is held in the collection of the Souls Grown Deep Foundation in Atlanta, Georgia. It stands 3.3 metres tall and is constructed from "things," including wood, steel, clothing, concrete, wire, oil cans, bottles, a glove, a number plate, found metal, paper collage, enamel, spray paint, and Splash Zone compound. At its base, a concrete garden statue of Pandora—the classical form recalibrated through the application of vivid yellow—represents and challenges hegemonic elite taste, as well as the objectification of female beauty. She stands atop a box plinth that recalls the Greek myth: after Prometheus stole fire from the gods and bestowed this power upon men, Zeus instructed the creation of the first woman, who was given a box she was told never to open. Defying this order to satisfy her curiosity, she opened the box and out came the troubles of the world, with hope trapped inside. Dial overshadows this double emblem of misogyny and systemic racism with a tower of materials, rising up, escaping, transforming, becoming . . .

We are living through reckonings with the past, our day-to-day lives transformed by global events. Looking through the pages of this book, the box remains an alternative space, filled to the brim with potential. Forget Pandora. The first box is that shoebox under your bed. In it, you can write your own history, lose yourself in the moment of making, and imagine a new future.

W A

1

T

E

R

LISA WOOLLETT
WHAT WE'VE THROWN AWAY

Born in London, Lisa Woollett grew up by the sea on the Isle of Sheppey, at the mouth of the River Thames. One of her favourite pastimes as a child was fossicking along the island's shores, collecting fossils and shark's teeth. The cliffs there are strange and otherworldly, constantly being eroded by the tides to the tune of about 1.5 metres a year. Lisa grew up with stories of local churches and pubs that, over time, had been lost to the sea; one such was "The Pub with No Beer," where the derelict remains of the gents were already halfway to the beach.

Lisa has spent her life mudlarking, collecting curious fragments of the past, from Roman tiles and Tudor thimbles to Victorian buttons and plastic soldiers. She sifts and sorts such items into ordered displays within old type cases, like exhibits in a museum of curiosities. This obsession is in the blood: her grandfather was a dustmen, while further back on her mother's side were the Tolladays, generations of scavengers, the lowest of the low of London's street life, scrounging a living from anything that had not been thrown into the Thames.

Through a series of walks beginning in central London, first to the Kentish estuary and eventually to Cornwall, Lisa has compiled a unique family memoir interwoven with social history. Called *Rag and Bone*, this muddy journey through time reveals the lives of "toshers" and shoremen, rag-and-bone families, men out collecting rubbish all day while the women and children raked through what came into the yard. Early Victorian London was essentially a zero-waste city: rags, paper, and scrap metal all had ready buyers; oyster shells went to builders for hardcore; vegetable matter was collected as pig food; and the ash that remained was bagged as fertilizer.

Lisa's book is a meditation on our relationship with objects—a portrait of what we were, and what we've become, before throwing things away became the great national pastime. From relics of Georgian empire-building and slave-trading, to Victorian London's barged-out refuse, to 1980s fly-tipping and the curse of present-day plastics, these stories of rubbish reveal our history of consumption. In 1997, for example, a container ship bound for New York pitched steeply and a cargo of 5 million pieces of Lego was dumped into the sea off Land's End. Ironically, many of the pieces were

Page 19
VINTAGE TOOTHBRUSHES,
HAIR CURLER PINS & COMBS

Opposite
GRADUAL BREAKDOWN OF
THE FLOTSAM ARMY

Above
TRAY OF PLASTIC FINDS
1950s/1960s to present day,
including two Lego dragons
(1997) and the lids of Smarties
tubes (1970s–2005)

from sea-themed play sets of divers and life rafts; twenty years later, they are still being found in the gullets of seabirds and the gills of fish.

Lisa, who is also an established photographer and author, currently lives with her family on the south coast of Cornwall, in a house full of buckets and boxes of beach and river finds.

SHORE FINDS
Objects collected while writing
Rag and Bone, *including:*

Action Man "hard hand"
(1966–1973)
Pewter blow-hole button
(1650–1700)
Bone comb (1600s–1700s)
Cycle reflector (came free
with box of Kellogg's Cornflakes
in 1989)

Bone toothbrush (c. 1800s)
Plastic ball from roll-on deodorant (2000s)
Lead toothpaste tubes (1800s–1900s)
Plastic wedding-cake dove (1970s–2000s)
Ring-type thimble (1450–1600)
Marlboro Man lighter (1970s–1900s)
Lego dragon (lost at sea in 1997)

Lead knight and horse's head (c. 1800s)
Turtle Wax air-freshener (1980s)
Disposable plastic razor and ice-cream spoon (1970s–2000s)
Marbles from Codd-neck bottles (c. 1800s)
Plastic cherub, dinosaurs, goat, and kangaroo (1970s–2000s)
Handmade pins (1400s–1700s)
Fragment of a delftware "scroll salt" (c. 1600s)

Ceramic doll parts (c. 1800s)
Light-bulb fittings (c. 1900s)
Plastic soldiers (1970s–2000s)
Brass toggle light switch (c. 1900s)
Death's head button moulds (c. 1700s)

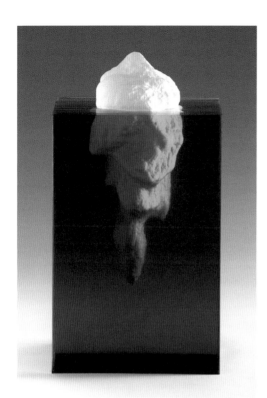

BEN YOUNG

A resident of Mount Maunganui, New Zealand, Ben Young is a self-taught artist who has been making glass sculptures for more than fifteen years, exhibiting internationally. Having spent most of his life living in the beautiful Bay of Plenty region on New Zealand's North Island, it seemed natural for him to take inspiration for his art from his local surroundings. A boat-builder by profession as well as a keen surfer, he is largely influenced by the sea and brings these passions together in his evocative glass forms. Ben's sculptures capture the ocean in its quiet moments, the solitude and humility one feels when confronted by something so immense and unyielding.

Each of Ben's works is drawn, cut, and crafted by hand from clear sheets of float glass before being laminated, layer upon layer, to create the final sculpture. Ben constructs models, draws templates, makes custom jigs, and then cuts the glass with a glazier's hand-tool. The complexity, says Ben, lies in the planning stage, during which there is much thinking before he can even start to draw or cut. After sketching the concept by hand, he creates a plan using traditional technical-drawing methods: "I work with 2D constructions and have to figure out how to translate that into a 3D finished piece. Sometimes my starting point changes dramatically as I have to find a way to layer the glass to create certain shapes.

"I decided early on that I was going to focus on this medium; having to work my ideas and techniques around these constraints appealed to me. Lighting plays a vital part in the presentation of my pieces. When lit from beneath, the light reflects, emanating its own life-force. I hope viewers might imagine the work as something 'living,' creating an illusion of space, movement, depth, and sense of spatial being. I like to play with the irony between the glass being a solid material and how I can form something so natural and organic."

ARCTIC "II"
2015, 20 × 30 × 20 cm
Laminated float glass

SUBTERRANEAN "II"
2015, 49 × 27 × 10cm
Laminated clear float glass
with cast concrete

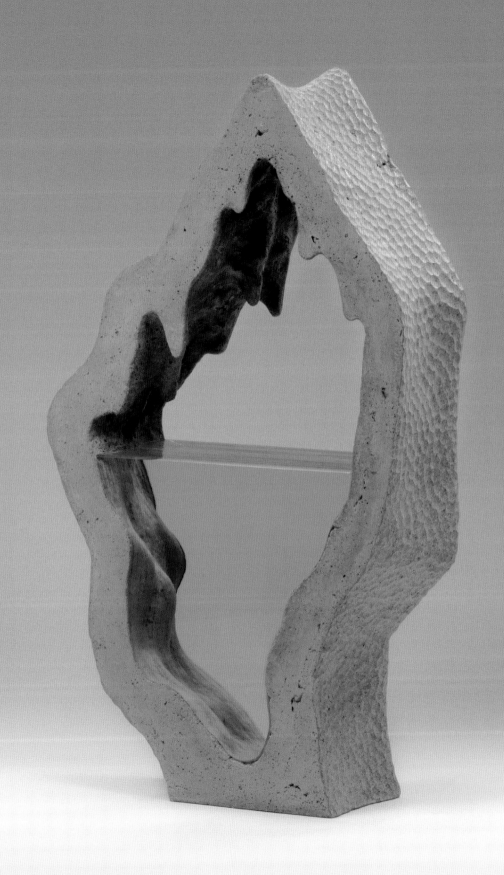

DAVID CASS

David Cass's artistic approach is wide-ranging, with each project anchored by sustainability and a concern for the environment. While painting and construction are the art forms he returns to most often, his recent projects have also embraced photography, writing, survey, and curation. Bound by their use of found and recycled materials, his award-winning artworks each investigate water in some way, from straight depictions of the sea and illustrations of rising sea levels to commentary on such extreme climatic events as the melting of the ice caps and participatory works involving his audience.

David believes wholeheartedly that art can serve as a beacon in this time of climate crisis. He has been in thrall to the wonder and beauty of the sea for as long as he can remember, struck by the mystery of the horizon. He rarely paints the sea from life, however, and suggests that his seascapes might be better described as abstract paintings, many derived from his imagination. Working in central Edinburgh, London, or Athens, David paints on such ordinary, everyday objects as matchboxes and tins, which he likes to think of as "trace fossils"—gathered surfaces, etched with evidence of life and time. He also paints on wooden doors, scored and scratched; drawers worn by daily use; ancient letters and postcards, written, sent, received, and kept. Through his use of such materials, the paintings

become a collaboration across time, carrying the marks of many hands. In addition, by using waste plastics or metals, including vintage advertisements for motor oil, he is able to imbue his works with his environmental concerns.

Among David's interests are the great floods of history, including the one that struck Florence in 1966. An article published in the flood's aftermath noted: "Nature will cooperate with man, if man learns to cooperate with Nature." Florence suffers a major flood roughly once every century, and some 2,500 square metres of frescoes in the city's central churches and museums have been badly damaged as a result. Art, says David, is a powerful tool in encouraging engagement with the environment—a notion that continually drives the artist forward.

Opposite top
MATCHBOX
2020, approx. 3.5 × 9 cm
Gouache on found material

Opposite bottom
PLATES BOX
2020, 9 × 9 × 2 cm
Gouache on found material

Above
SO MANY ENDINGS II
2012–13, 39 × 39 × 10 cm
Gouache on objects and collected offcuts

"Rituals performed in private change
the face of the world."
Roger Ackling

RICHARD JOHNSON

The late Richard Johnson used large-format digital photography to document the structures that shape our cultures and communities, preserving such places in a rapidly shifting world. Inspired by the work of mid-twentieth-century German photographers Bernd and Hilla Becher, Richard's *Ice Huts* series records the temporary ice-fishing huts and villages that populate many Canadian waterways during the winter. In tightly cropped compositions, Richard fixes his lens on the formal and material qualities of the architecture and examines its relationship to site, revealing the creativity, character, and humour of these hideaways.

Each of the structures in the series glows with an aura of wonder and rustic significance. Born of a need for sustenance, ice fishing was handed down from such indigenous peoples as the Inuit, whose lives depended on the scant resources offered by an apparently inhospitable landscape. But even for Richard's modern-day hinterland voyagers, the basics remain the same: the huts have openings in the floor, and the fishermen must cut holes in the ice, the size varying depending on whether they are using a line or a spear.

With a background in commercial interior design, Richard was attracted to architectural photography by the simplicity of these renegade, folk-art constructions. "It is architecture at its most

primitive level," he says. "It's shelter. It's portable. It's made by the owners of the hut. It's not pretentious. It is a solution. Every single person needs heat." Of his photographs of the huts, he says: "For me, these are really portraits of the individual. But the individual is not present."

Each year, entire ice-fishing villages are abandoned as the ice melts, only to be reconstituted the following year. Unseasonally high temperatures can sometimes drive the same villages onto a farmer's field or open ground—groups of huts with cows and rabbits instead of fish and ice. Richard described these gatherings as "ice villages on holiday."

"Preserving, holding, protecting; building, dwelling, thinking. The hut may be, after it's humble fashion, the most essential building we mortals can know. Within it's tiny confines, the whole world awaits."
Mark Kingwell, Professor of Philosophy, University of Toronto

29

JULIE SPEED

To quote the artist herself, Julie Speed is a "para-realist": although her works are strange and fantastical, the situations they depict are not wholly inconceivable. A self-taught artist who lives and works in Marfa, Texas—a small desert city with a big art scene—Julie is also a careful student of such diverse subjects as mythology, Russian religious icons, and Mughal and Aboriginal art. Her works are an intriguing blend of these disparate and seemingly incongruent influences. Another source of inspiration was her great-aunt Phyllis, a palmist who travelled the globe between the world wars gathering and translating traditional fairy tales and reading the translations to Julie. Replete with otherworldly characters and dark, surreal storylines, such fairy tales had a profound impact on the young artist.

Collecting is at the heart of Julie's practice, working as she does with a vast store of found materials and random ephemera, whether maps of the constellations or taxonomic prints. Describing her art, she has said: "composition comes first." Getting it right is also of utmost importance: if a collage element is not working, she will replace it or else find a different way forward. "While I rarely get there," she acknowledges, "my aim is always to find that certain arrangement that takes me for a moment behind the veil." It is being inside and fully occupied by the work that keeps any anxieties at bay, the deep concentration involved in the process of making that keeps the monsters under the bed.

There is a physical presence to Julie's work that draws you in, challenging your own experiences, knowledge, and prejudices as you endeavour to interpret their meaning. "My thoughts, even my really, really deep thoughts, about [my works] carry no more weight than anyone else's," says Julie. Among her many observations about the world, Julie believes that the contrast between the perfect geometry of the universe and the lunacy of man is irreconcilable.

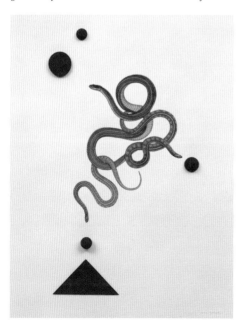

A childhood memory reveals a little more about the thinking behind Julie's practice: "My father built ship models from scratch. Beneath the deck, hidden inside the hold of one of my favourite models, is a ladder leading down to the ship's galley, where a tiny drunken captain sits slumped over in his chair holding a bottle of rum. Lying across the table in front of him, with her head in her hands, is a naked woman. The lighter part of the carved wood is her skin and the darker part is her hair. The whole thing is only about an inch or so across. Once the deck housing is back in place, no one will ever see it. He carved it because he wanted to and he could. Sometimes it's just that simple."

PIANO
2015, 17.3 × 13.3 × 3 cm
Collage, gouache, postage
stamp, and steel

MAN IN AN IRON MASK
2015, 17.3 × 12 × 3 cm
Found paper, iron, wood,
and glass eye

TRICK SNAKES (detail)
2007, 76.2 × 55.9 cm
Collage, gouache, and wood

CYRUS KABIRU

Cyrus Kabiru was born in Nairobi, Kenya, where he currently lives and works as a self-taught artist. A self-proclaimed flâneur and collector of Nairobi's junk, he's a true believer in "giving trash a second chance." Cyrus repurposes and refashions found materials into one-of-a-kind commodity objects. Utensils, wood, wires, bottle caps, and other rejected items make him feel like "a warrior of nature," helping the environment through recycling.

Cyrus is probably best known for his "Black Mamba" series of old bicycles and his "C-Stunners"—an ongoing project in which the artist creates and wears artistic bifocals. His intricate sculptural works push the boundaries of conventional craftsmanship, sculpture, and fashion, as well as portraying the aspirations of "bling" youth culture and his nation's resourcefulness. For Cyrus, the collections are also personal, not least his

2020 radio series. Cyrus's grandfather was the first person in his village to own a radio, and the artist recalls all the villagers coming to listen to it; that radio was then passed down to his father and, in turn, to Cyrus and his brothers. Once in his possession, Cyrus added FM to the radio's limited medium- and short-wave capacity. It was this upgrade that inspired the artist to use discarded radios in his work.

Cyrus's mantra is to give new life to old things and "work hard, work smart." In February 2020, he opened a visual-arts space near Thika, a town to the northeast of Nairobi, in which his fellow artists could create and exhibit their work.

BED BUGS
2020, 45 × 45 × 15 cm
Steel and found objects

PORTRAIT OF ARTIST
IN C-STUNNERS

OLD YOGA
2020, 40 × 40 × 12 cm
Steel and found objects

MIYALE YA BLUE
2020, 60 × 65 × 15 cm
Steel and found objects

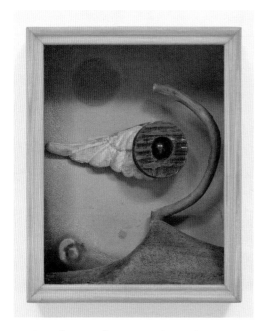

DAVE MOORE

Dave Moore moved to Hayling Island in Hampshire as a child, and has lived in the same house ever since. He spent most of his working life as a self-employed fisherman, becoming increasingly interested in the "alien" catches in his lobster pots, such as random bronze artefacts and ancient pieces of wood.

Although he worked mainly as a fisherman, Dave often took on other marine-related jobs, sometimes with colourful results. On one occasion, he was manoeuvring a yacht so its mast could be removed when the mast touched an overhead power line. While Dave survived what was a very powerful electric shock, probably thanks to the rubber gloves he was wearing, the incident caused a power cut that affected the military inhabitants of nearby Thorney Island. In the early 1970s Dave was in his "office"—the Yew Tree pub—when he received a visit from Scotland Yard in relation to fitting out a boat. The boat in question was to be used as a pirate radio station by the people responsible for filming the 1970 Isle of Wight festival. Dave was arrested and later released without charge. He still believes to this day that he is listed by the police as an "undesirable person."

One of Dave's principal influences as an artist was the modernist designer and painter John Tunnard, some of whose works he saw during a trip to Cornwall to buy some second-hand lobster pots; another was the surrealism of Eileen Agar. After retiring from the sea in 2007, Dave began enjoying long beachcombing walks on the Hayling Island foreshore. He clearly remembers the creation of his first box, which was based on two pieces of driftwood. They reminded him of a princess and a frog, and he wanted to imply that the frog was gifting a collection of jewels to the princess.

TO THE AVIONS WHO NEVER MADE
IT PAST THE CONTROL TOWER
2010, 21.5 × 17 × 7.6 cm
*Shoreline finds with decalcomania-
painted background*

I HAVE NO RESERVATIONS
2009, 27 × 18 × 9 cm
*Shoreline finds with decalcomania-
painted background*

SILENT NIGHT
2012, 72 × 66 × 16.5 cm
*Driftwood construction with
decalcomania-painted base*

KIM KEEVER
AQUATIC ABSTRACTIONS

The Miami-based artist Kim Keever once worked at NASA as a
thermal engineer, researching how fluids bypass solid objects at
high speeds. Experimenting with paint and balloons underwater,
Kim continues to explore this scientific and investigative aspect
of his personality by conjuring his very own odes to physics. At
the heart of his studio is a 200-gallon water tank that serves as his
canvas; the countless empty bottles of paint strewn on the floor are
his paintbrushes.

    Kim creates vibrant abstractions by squeezing differently
coloured paints into the water tank. The paints swirl around
one another and form shifting clouds of colour, which he then
photographs with a 100-megapixel camera, using lights and
colourful gels for enhanced effect. Kim claims that the most
fascinating part of the process is the pouring of the paint into
the water, since no two occasions yield the same results. The
explosive shapes and forms are remarkably photogenic despite the
haphazard process. "I love the randomness," he says.
"I have no idea what the paint is going to do, what colours
are really going to be prominent in the outcome." Some
pigments, like house paint, sink like rocks to the bottom
of the tank; others, such as ink, drizzle slowly through the
water, creating thin, airy, billowing strips of colour.

STUDIO VIEW, MIAMI, 2021

ABSTRACT 14718
2014, 68 × 61 cm/127 × 117 cm
Edition prints
Paint in 200-gallon water tank

Kim has come a long way since his first creative endeavours: making enamel-painted balsa-wood planes with his father, an aircraft engineer. Stirred by Picasso's wild spirit, he greatly admires Roxy Paine's installations and Cindy Sherman's singular use of photography. Since becoming a full-time artist, Kim's paint panoramas have attracted worldwide attention, leading to collaborative projects with singer-songwriter Joanna Newsom and film-maker Paul Thomas Anderson.

Full of momentous energy frozen in time, Kim's compositions recall planets, atoms, and stars—worlds within worlds that could well be biblical. They also echo the work of the German Romantic painters, as well as suggesting the more ominous force and vision of a Cormac McCarthy novel. Kim's intention, he says, is to present the landscape as beauty itself, without reference to man or industry. Often he incorporates whichever materials he can find—whether on the street, in stores, or on the internet—that might amplify the suggestion that all is not quite what it seems. The Hudson River School is most often associated with his work, owing to the idyllic quality and dreamy hues of the vistas; for his part, Kim favours a line from a review of his work by Kit White: "There were mountains, sunsets and ocean shores before there were eyes to see them." Science with a little imagination can certainly go a long way.

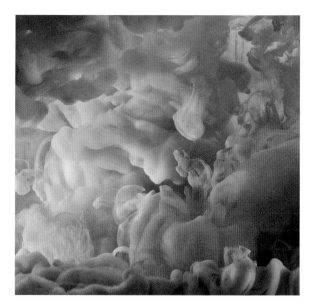

ABSTRACT 10166 (detail)
2014, 61 × 68.5 cm/109 × 122 cm
Edition prints
Paint in 200-gallon water tank

ABSTRACT 46683
2019, 71 × 71 cm/112 × 112 cm
Edition prints
Paint in 200-gallon water tank

WEST 150K
2010, 71 × 71 cm/127 × 127 cm
Edition prints
Plaster, paint in 200-gallon water tank

Pages 40–41
TURTLE SKULL ROCK
2001, 78 × 117 cm/101 × 152 cm
Edition prints
Plaster, paint in 200-gallon water tank

"On a three-dimensional scale, I think of these spaces
as containing endless universes becoming smaller and
smaller. The same is true in the opposite direction. Our
universe is contained by other universes and those are
contained by more universes ad infinitum."
Kim Keever

KATHARINE MORLING

Katharine Morling is best known for her life-sized black-and-white sculptures of domestic objects, or, as she calls them, three-dimensional drawings in ceramic. Although she calls herself a "3D person," drawing is very important to Katharine. On the surface, her sculptures can be seen as sketches of inanimate objects; when considered more closely, however, they become new life forms, making us question materiality and functionality. From the most ordinary of everyday objects, the artist creates animated tableaux, alluding to stories, dreams, and the uncanny.

The monochrome works are mainly porcelain or crank, covered in a black porcelain slip—used to pick out such details as a handle or a lock—and then kiln-fired. Rafts of drawings begin the process, based on emotions and experiences, until one grabs the artist's imagination sufficiently to warrant the next stage. Based on detailed research, the sculpting is intricate and time-consuming, sometimes involving up to three assistants working alongside Katharine in her London studio. While exhibiting her work worldwide, she has also created pieces for permanent display, such as a series of mythological creatures—on view in Stoke-on-Trent—produced in response to the Staffordshire Hoard.

BOOM
2018, 40 × 43 × 15 cm
Porcelain and black stain

NEST BOX
2018, 25 × 40 × 23 cm
Antique box, porcelain, and black stain

PLENTY
2011, 45 × 50 × 50 cm
Porcelain and black stain

DAVID BRAY

David Bray is something of a sensory renaissance man, drawn to his immediate surroundings or whatever comes to hand. His father used to work at the Royal Academy of Arts in London, and would occasionally allow David and his brother to wander free among the masters and national treasures before the galleries opened to the public. It was after one of these visits that David knew he wanted to become an artist.

As a child, David would draw images of space travel, portraying himself and his friends visiting other planets. After becoming a successful illustrator, he began to develop a distinctive, delicate style using pencils, pens, inks, and paints. Inspired by such figures as Allen Jones and Helmut Newton, the drawings he produced were often worlds rooted in dark fantasy and erotic beauty.

Frequently entwined among the playful and voyeuristic in David's work is his use of words—his own unique syntax, which can be at once brilliant, absurd, and downright dangerous. His work is restlessly versatile and always evolving, spanning a range of creative styles depending on his environment. The decision to move out of London to the Kent countryside proved a seismic shift, exposing him to nature, open space, and the changing seasons. Picking up his late father's set of watercolours, David began creating landscapes, soon experimenting with oils. There is a Turner-esque dreaminess to these works, which can be serene and ominously beautiful.

Many of David's creations reflect a compulsion to collect and assemble; even the paintings feel like inverted trays. All the works shown here are made from some form of reclaimed wooden packaging,

dismantled and reconfigured into "traditional" art shapes. *The Tiger*, for example, was inspired by some old puppets that once belonged to his grandparents. Working indoors, David has to avoid painting on a pair of overly inquisitive cats—an animal type to which he is clearly drawn.

RETURN OF THE RETURNER
2019, 25 × 19 × 5 cm
Acrylic on wood panel, framed in
reclaimed tray panel

I LOVE YOU MORE THAN SPINACH
2018, 21 × 15 × 4 cm
Household emulsion and pen on
reclaimed panel

PERSONAL DELIVERY
2017, 21 × 9 × 8 cm
Household emulsion on found wood

SEAN MADDEN

"My world is a beautifully ridiculous place full of contradiction, confusing boundaries, old traditions, and new technologies."

Sean Madden lives on the south coast of England, where he has been contributing to the local art scene for more than two decades. Primarily a painter, producing works in an abstract expressionist style, he also makes original sculpture—inventions with a hint of the darkly surreal using an endless array of resources. Along with employing recycled materials, Sean has a passion for trawling through junk shops for the unloved, for objects that can be rethought and recycled, breathing new life into old forms.

Sean's influences include pop culture, science fiction, classical mythology, and the avant-garde, as well as the English comic-book illustrator Kevin O'Neill. Originally, *The Brighton and Hove Walker* was conceived as an alternative to the then unconstructed British Airways i360, now a famous landmark on the East Sussex coast. The work took its inspiration from an electric railway invented by Magnus Volk that opened on the Brighton seafront in 1896. Billed as "A Sea Voyage on Wheels," Volk's remarkable creation consisted of a single carriage—known as "Daddy Long Legs"—that carried sightseers through the shallows atop four, 7-metre-high legs. Also drawing on the world of *Star Wars*, Sean went about building his own steam-powered version, complete with background story, promotional posters, and even tickets for the daily fictional ride. Among his other works that reference the local area is *I Love You*, inspired by Graham Greene's 1938 novel *Brighton Rock*.

I LOVE YOU
2012, 24 × 24 × 5 cm
Engraved razor in frame

MECHANICAL HEART
2013, 40 × 25 cm
Assorted metal and plastic,
glass bell jar

THE BRIGHTON AND HOVE
WALKER
2013, 80 × 60 × 18 cm
Recycled plastic and tin toys

VIARCO

Founded in 1907, Viarco is not only the oldest but also the only pencil manufacturer in Portugal. Based in São João da Madeira, near the coastal city of Porto, this family-owned business uses the highest-quality graphite, carbon, and binders to produce art materials—from pencils and watercolours to putties, crayons, and paints—that are considered to be some of the best in the world. Daniel Sommer's insightful portraits provide a unique glimpse inside the factory as well as of its products.

Daniel's photographs present the manufacturing process as an art form in its own right. Viarco has always drawn on its legacy: old but trusted machinery, Portuguese culture, craftsmanship, and proud and faithful employees. There is no such position as technician or mechanic at the company; instead, all the workers are capable of repairing the machines themselves—not that there is anyone around anymore who could be employed with such skills. Improvisation is also common; in one part of the factory, for example, a baker's dough-maker has been re-purposed as a high-quality colour-mixer.

The Viarco brand—now more than a hundred years old—is both ancient and modern at the same time. By remaining passionate about its work, the company has found a way to preserve its heritage while also pursuing new paths. After all, pencils, as they say, are the seeds to all ideas.

Photography by Daniel Sommer

ANNA BARLOW

"It is the juxtaposition of temporary ice cream and permanent ceramics that inspires me to produce one in the other. To solidify a fleeting, melting moment and highlight a relationship between the soft and the solid. The rituals and culture around the eating of sweet food continue to fascinate me. An undercurrent of competitiveness, anxiety, consumerism, and performance is usually lurking beneath the surface of a three-tiered ombre butter cream piñata cake."

Anna Barlow is a British artist who is known internationally for her realistic and visually stunning ceramic sculptures of ice cream, cakes, and other sweet foods—sculptures that she uses to tell stories about and build a fantasy around food. Using actual cake-decorating tools, Anna has developed an extraordinary ability to combine traditional techniques with her own methods. She focuses on ice cream as it is such a momentary yet memorable treat that most of us have experienced, evoking vivid memories and desired indulgences. She uses many types of clay, from a low-firing white earthenware and a high-fired black clay to beautiful translucent bone china. Such materials lend a "visual edibility" to her work; it is up to the imagination of the viewer to decide how they will taste. Anna enjoys the serenity of her London studio on City Island, where she absorbs the changing tides and light over the River Thames, surrounded by the vibrant colours of Lego-like architecture.

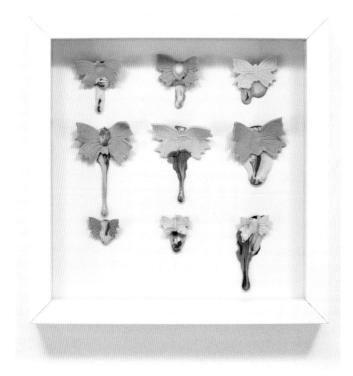

AFTER THE PARTY
2013, 20 × 17 × 25 cm
Ceramic, glaze, silver-plated spoon, and adhesive

SQUISHED
2013, 25 × 25 × 4 cm
Porcelain, glaze, adhesive, and picture frame

BONNIE & CLYDE

Steph Burnley, aka Bonnie & Clyde, is a Brighton-based mixed-media artist, working primarily in collage, photography, and print. Taking inspiration from music, film, nostalgic iconography, and urban spaces, her work interweaves aspects of the current sociopolitical climate with emotional and more personal themes. Travel plays a huge part in her art: as each image is distorted, cut, and layered, Steph creates bizarre, far-off places that still retain an element of familiarity and warmth. The iconic topography of California—from the vibrant architecture of Santa Monica to rows of palm trees at Venice Beach—feature heavily in her imaginary scenes, while street photography, architecture, and seascape imagery also play a key role in her aesthetic. With a visual cocktail of photographer

Helen Levitt and artist David Hockney, Steph explores the relationship between the built environment and the natural landscape to dizzying effect. Armed with her Leica camera and jet-set spirit, she can take you to Tokyo, London, or Havana, on tours of the endless psychogeography of the metropolis.

PLAY CHILE
2012, 21.5 × 15 × 6.5 cm
Collage assemblage in cigar box

ICE CREAM TEARS
2012, 15 × 12 × 5 cm
Collage assemblage in cigar box

KURT TONG
IN CASE IT RAINS IN HEAVEN

Born in Hong Kong in 1977, Kurt Tong trained as a health visitor at the University of Liverpool before working in and travelling across Europe, the Americas, and Asia. In 1999, Kurt co-founded Prema Vasam, a charitable home for disabled and disadvantaged children in Chennai, South India. He became a full-time photographer in 2003, winning the Luis Valtueña International Humanitarian Photography Award with his first picture story documenting the treatment of disabled children in India. After gaining his master's in documentary photography, he began working on much more personal projects exploring his Chinese roots and an understanding of his motherland.

Tong's series *In Case It Rains in Heaven* is a modern-day portrait of the centuries-old Chinese funerary tradition of making joss-paper offerings to the dead. Many Chinese people believe that, when a person dies, they leave this life with no earthly possessions, and that it is up to their descendants to provide for them in the next. This age-old practice can be traced back to the burying of grave goods in Neolithic times. Originally, coins and animals were buried with the dead, but when that proved too expensive for commoners, they began burning joss paper decorated with seals, stamps, or silver or gold paint, as offerings to the spirits to ensure they lived well in the hereafter. Some say this "ghost money" could be used by the dead to bribe their way to a swifter reincarnation. Over the years, the paper offerings have become much more elaborate, from a bird in a bamboo cage representing the traditional to the modern consumerism of laptops, McDonald's, and Louis Vuitton bags. Yet many items may also be aspirational: an aeroplane, for example, might be intended not for a multimillionaire but for someone who has never flown.

Following the recent political unrest in Hong Kong and the Covid-19 pandemic, joss-paper helmets, replicas of the heavy-duty masks worn by protesters, and colourful PPE now join the catalogue of

offerings to accompany the city's loved ones on their journey to the next life. There are now even websites that allow bereaved relatives to select digital items for online burning. Tong's vibrant photos explore how an ancient tradition reflects the materialism of Asia's rapidly developing economy in an increasingly westernized society. Many observers say that young people have little interest in this tradition, but Kurt is not so sure: "I think people don't believe in this until their loved ones pass away."

Left, opposite, and pages 54–55
AN ASSORTMENT OF
JOSS-PAPER OBJECTS

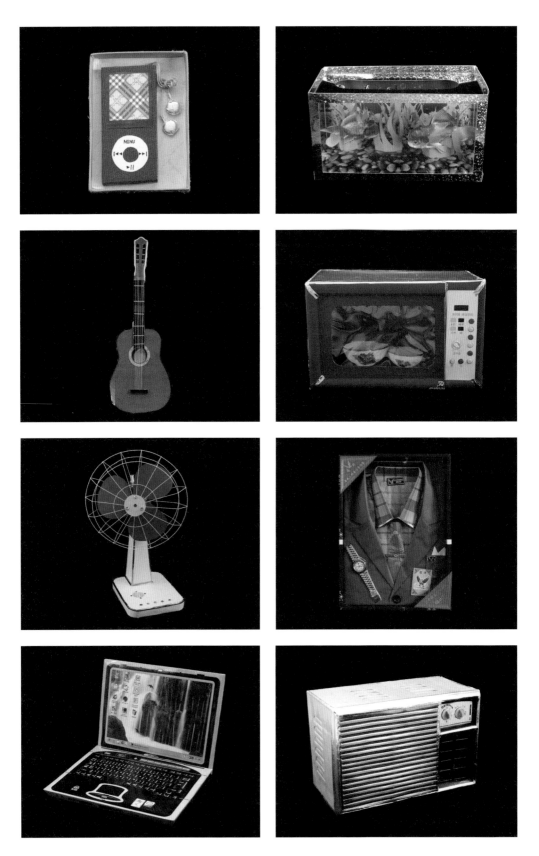

Kurt's *Patriotic Smoking* is a series of photographs of cigarettes produced in North Korea. The cigarettes were purchased on the black market at the border town of Dandong in China.

While it is believed that smoking is common among North Korean men of all social classes, there have been recent reports that Kim Jong-un has ordered his officials not to smoke foreign-produced cigarettes and to show their patriotic loyalty by smoking only locally produced products. The cigarette packets featured in Kurt's photographs bear such life-affirming names as "Heavenly Lake," "Luminous," "Dawn," "Beautiful Land," and "Dragon Mountain."

There are fourteen cigarette factories in North Korea, producing dozens of different brands. However, they remain beyond the reach of most people in the country, who smoke hand-rolled cigarettes using the local newspaper.

The images in Kurt's series, taken in a simple "pack shot" style, are not intended to make a sweeping statement about life in North Korea; nor are they a commentary on smoking. Instead, they give the viewer a chance to experience the advertising, branding, and design style of a highly secretive country.

PATRIOTIC SMOKING
2016, mixed formats

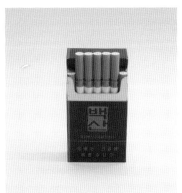

ANYA BEAUMONT

Anya Beaumont is an artist, cartographer, and lecturer. Having grown up in the rural north of England before moving to Manchester and then London, changes in her environment have been a significant factor in her practice. Within her observations of place, an interest in contemporary life sits alongside musings on Britain's architectural heritage. *Growth* is the central work in a series of hand-cut paper sculptures developed from observations of decorative architectural features on nineteenth-century buildings in London. Initially used as a prop in photographs documenting contrasts in the built environment, it grew and changed into an entity in its own right—something between an architectural detail and a more organic, moss-like form.

Growth is made from recycled paper collected in Kilburn, north London, the location that inspired it. *Hera's Garden* evolved from studies of the sumptuous interiors of Corsham Court in Wiltshire, close to where Anya now lives. Many of the plaster ceilings in the house were designed by the famous landscape architect Capability Brown, who also designed the grounds. In classical mythology, Hera was given a tree that bore sacred golden apples, guarded in her orchard by nymphs. It was the combination of baroque riches and nature in both Hera's story and the house, explains Anya, that led her to the work's title. She adds that sometimes, when she catches a glimpse of the work, she can see a nymph in it too.

Responding to the climate crisis, Anya has expanded her research interests to include the natural world. She also continues to use recycled paper and plastics in her work.

Above
HERA'S GARDEN
2019, 48 × 28 × 6 cm
Painted hand- and laser-cut paper sculpture in bespoke frame

Opposite (detail left)
GROWTH
2014, 120 × 120 × 4.5 cm
Hand-cut paper sculpture in frame

LARA HAILEY

Based in the UK, Lara Hailey is a multidisciplinary artist who often works with textiles. Over the course of her career, she has made a number of quilts that use text to tell the stories of both groups and individuals. Inspiration has come from a range of sources, from text messages left at the end of a relationship to the response of her local community to the London riots of 2011. Indeed, one of her most moving works is *We Love Peckham* (2012), a huge patchwork quilt made up of fabric Post-it notes expressing locals' reactions to the rioting. To create the work, Lara photographed the original Post-its, which had been stuck to the window of a shop in Peckham in the aftermath of the riots, and transferred the text onto 400 pieces of fabric before stitching them together. She is interested in using quilts—symbols of comfort and homeliness—as vehicles for personal expression and as ways to document social histories.

Sewn Antidote is a collaborative quilt made in response to the Covid-19 pandemic and the effects of being in isolation. The work was conceived and designed by Lara at the beginning of the first lockdown out of a desire to keep people connected through a communal stitching project, like a virtual sewing circle. Contributors were asked to provide a circular design and to stick to a particular colour scheme; most importantly, they were encouraged to express their own experiences of the pandemic and of being in isolation. As a result, the designs are extremely diverse: some give thanks to the NHS and key workers; some express emotions and sentiments provoked by loneliness and separation; some tell of the activities that kept their creators busy; while others tackle societal and political issues linked to the pandemic, such as the death toll, homelessness, and the failings of political leaders. Together, the designs provide a poignant and comprehensive response to the impact of the pandemic and lockdown. They are also a tribute to the inventiveness of the contributors. One used nuts and bolts to represent Covid, while another appliquéd a sheet of toilet paper with the words, "Unpick . . . in case of emergency." *Sewn Antidote* is now in the fashion and textile collection of the Victorian and Albert Museum.

SEWN ANTIDOTE
2020, 195 × 195 cm
Machine-quilted organdie on canvas
with 90 appliquéd roundels

LORRAINE CLARKE

Lorraine Clarke's work takes multiple forms, from large installations to small, finely crafted collections, incorporating found and made objects, text, animation, and sound, all infused with an interest in rites and traditions, belief systems, religion, anthropology, and aspects of the medical world and the human condition. Like the practices of a white witch, her creative process has a plant-like quality, absorbing energy from materials and making them bud, branch, and bloom. In Lorraine's hands, what some might regard as detritus is transformed into serious objects of contemplation—strange and new yet somehow familiar—challenging us to reflect on what it is to be human. Plant roots, flotsam, and weathered plastics are fastidiously framed, caged, and shaped into new specimens that force the viewer to question what is organic, manufactured, or magical. *That Tribal Sense of Self*, for example, is a fantastical display of bottled specimens, like a great library of medicaments from a medieval apothecary.

Since 2002, Lorraine has created a large body of work expressing her ongoing interest in the link between magic, medicine, and religion, from primitive times to the modern day. The works embody insights from the "wise women" of the pre-modern era to contemporary ethical concerns, and address issues common to every culture and age, such as identity, fertility, faith, sexuality, and mortality. Her current practice is informed by developments in biotechnology, including organ harvesting and cloning, and the enormous complexity of the psyche. Central to Lorraine's work are the notions of hope, kinship, healing, and the preciousness and precariousness of life, as well as laughter. After living and working in Italy for nineteen years, Lorraine returned to the UK to found Euroart Studios in London.

EX VOTO
(BODY BOX)
2008, 28 × 30 × 4.5 cm
Ceramic assemblage in box

STORM DROPPINGS
2009, 33 × 29 × 5 cm
Mixed-media installation

THAT TRIBAL
SENSE OF SELF
2011, 225 × 158 × 48 cm
Mixed-media installation

ANNE WHITE

For Anne White, early inspiration came from Bill Bryson's book *At Home: A Short History of Private Life*, which describes chamber pots being stored in sideboards in dining rooms and kettles doubling as bedpans in bedrooms. A collection of blue-and-white china and enamelware soon became the beginnings of a new body of work, with the working title "In One End, Out the Other." The series explores containers that can be used at either end of the body, receptacles that mediate between the body and its functions . . . For Anne, everything in the world is a medium to be used in her art.

Anne's work is concerned not only with such formal matters as material, surface, and form, but also with more abstract concepts, such as the border between inside and outside, the public and the private, questioning our psychological boundaries when faced with life's leftovers. "The abject," says the French philosopher Julia Kristeva, is "both repellent and seductive." It is the inevitable, push–pull feeling of abjection, of being at once repelled and seduced, that is at the heart of Anne's work and the humour it contains.

A number of Anne's pieces are enveloped in meticulously stitched silk velvet, revealing only a glimpse of what is contained within and enticing the viewer to look closer. The silver christening set *Lanugo* is a sensory reminder of a child's unease when exploring the world. These and other works are often displayed in direct relation to specific regions of the body: *Jugs*, for example, is positioned at chest height, while *Deadpan*, evocative of a coffin, sits on the floor, a reminder of our inevitable decline. Anne studied fine art at the University of Chichester, where she is currently teaching to all ages while exploring materials and researching new work.

DEADPAN
2013, 18 × 50 × 42 cm
Enamel bedpan, foam,
silk velvet, powder-
coated MDF

LANUGO
2013, 20 × 18 × 3 cm
Silver christening set,
flocked with nylon
fibres

JUGS
2014, 28 × 20 × 37 cm
Pair of Spode cream
jugs, foam, stitched silk
velvet, MDF

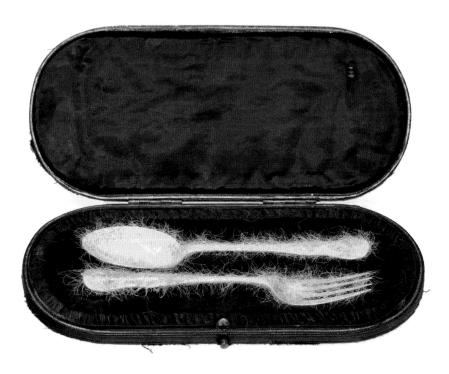

"Fur may delight the touch, but it repels the tongue"
Meret Oppenheim, surrealist

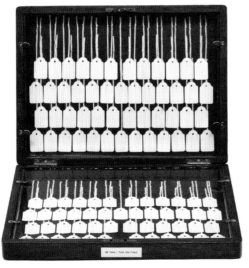

MELANIE WARD

Through her work, Melanie Ward seeks to balance feelings of loss, emptiness, and isolation with a sense of anonymity and distance, concentrating on subjects such as loneliness and relationship breakdown. In *200 Opportunities I Missed*, 200 small pen drawings are displayed within a repurposed cutlery box. Ward meticulously drew repeating rhythmic lines onto small labels as a way to symbolize missed opportunities and explore the resultant feelings of loss and despair.

While this and similar works were initially created for highly personal reasons, their final display is deliberately detached: the small drawings are carefully presented behind glass, creating distance between the viewer and the work's biographical nature. This separation gives the work an untouchable quality, something to be observed from afar as the layers of emotional meaning are purposefully concealed. Likewise, the use of a box allows the artist to close the lid and suspend these emotions temporarily.

200 Opportunities I Missed suggests the way in which we compartmentalize and simplify our experiences. *99 Times I Tried and Failed* deals with a similar theme, with the experiences that gave rise to it reduced to stark, black-and-white pen drawings, intentionally lacking in colour. Melanie's projects use drawing, collage, video, print, and sculpture, often incorporating repetition or taking the form of a series. Over the last decade, she has worked as a freelance artist in the film industry, making and painting props for special effects.

Top
200 OPPORTUNITIES I MISSED
2014, 35 × 25.5 × 6 cm
200 pen-drawn labels, glass, wooden box

Above (detail left)
99 TIMES I TRIED AND FAILED
2014, 35 × 25.5 × 6 cm
99 pen-drawn labels, glass, wooden box

JULIA MADDISON

"The room was in a house full of heavy, stolid things with white sheets thrown over them. Blinds were drawn, doors shut, defending against light and air. A man in his sixties lived in the house, creeping amid masses and shadows. He used almost nothing, apparently, and kept things undisturbed, hidden, as if waiting for the true owner of the house to return and pull away the sheets, use the furniture, live here."
From Sylvia *by Leonard Michaels*

BLUSH
2014, 10 × 8 × 2 cm
Found cigarette case, textile scrap, photocopy, gouache, and pencil

This extract could well provide the setting for one of Julia Maddison's installations. Julia's work revolves around secrets, sex, sickness, loss, and lies. She collects, reworks, and subverts the flotsam of forgotten lives, creating different narratives out of misremembered histories. By piecing together scraps, fripperies, and unwanted ephemera, often incorporating her own drawings, photographs, erratic sewing, or peculiar constructions, she gradually builds a kind of museum of domestic misery. In the words of Samuel Beckett, "Nothing is funnier than unhappiness."

After years of scrabbling about in an unheated house, without hot water, in one of the least glamorous parts of far-flung north London, slaking her thirst only with the dubious wines at obscure private views, Julia has recently escaped to the coast in search of solitude and space. She is, she says, always searching for something.

On the subject of boxes, Julia tells the story of the biscuit tin in which Louise Bourgeois's mother had kept the tapestry male genitalia she'd had to cut out of the antique tapestries she was restoring for rich but puritanical Americans. Louise's task was to design appropriately shaped foliage to fill the holes where the mighty manhoods of Greek mythology had once been on show.

Despite claiming to have retired to the British seaside, Julia continues to exhibit and curate exhibitions in London. Among her recent projects are *The Drinker's Body*, an installation about despair created with Matthew Tudor and held in a derelict house in Peckham; and *Mother's Ruin*, a group exhibition in a former gin distillery in east London. She has also been working on a film: a brief, quixotic adventure based on stories of her unknown travelling-carpet-salesman birth father. It is also Julia's long-held ambition to run a shop similar to the one in the animated children's television series *Bagpuss*—full of found oddments, discarded fragments, and personal ephemera, none of which is for sale.

Above
MUMMY IS SAD
2014, 20 × 40 × 23 cm
Wooden box, textiles, paper,
and pencil

Opposite, clockwise from top left
HIDE & SEEK
2014, 15 × 20.5 × 3 cm
Butter-knife box, photograph,
mask

THE BATHERS
2017, 8 × 11 × 2.5 cm
Vintage tobacco tin,
photograph, tea towel

COUGH CONTROL
2020, 6.5 × 8.3 × 1.5 cm
Vintage Tussils tin, still
from Andrei Tarkovsky's film
Andrei Rublev

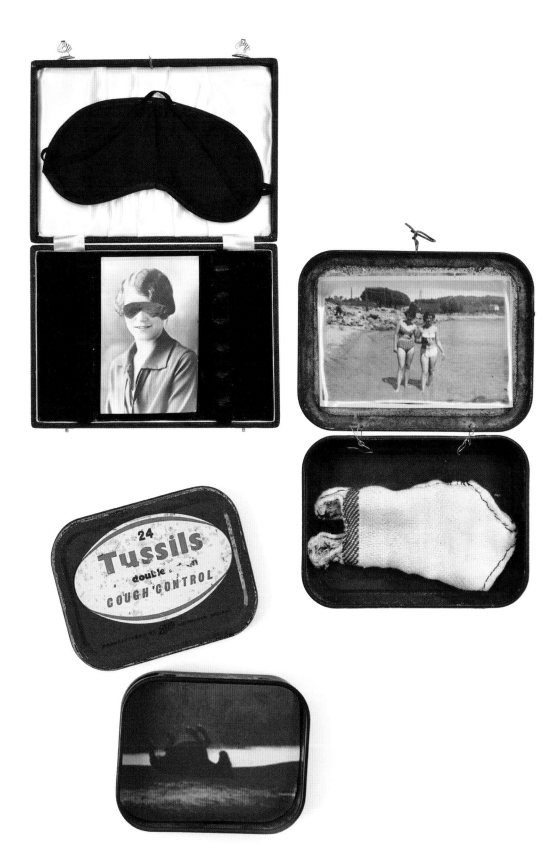

MOHAMED HAFEZ
PORTALS TO A GOLDEN AGE

hiraeth (n.), a homesickness for a home to which you cannot return, a home that maybe never was; the nostalgia, the yearning, the grief for the lost places of your past.

Mohamed Hafez is a Syrian American artist and architect. Born in Damascus, he was raised in the Kingdom of Saudi Arabia and educated in the Midwestern United States. When he first moved to America from Syria, not long after the events of 9/11, a fear of Islam and Muslims was at its peak. President George W. Bush's travel regulations were targeting Muslim-majority countries, while Syrians were being lumped in with other Muslims, indistinguishable in the American mind.

In recent years, Syria has been rocked by a bloody civil war. The atrocities of the conflict are reflected in Mohamed's art through his use of found objects, such as paint and scrap metal. Making the most of his architectural skills, he creates surrealistic Middle Eastern streetscapes depicting cities besieged by war, capturing the magnitude of the devastation and highlighting the fragility of human life. In deliberate contrast to the violence of war, however, his art takes hope from the richness of thousands of years of history as well as verses from the Qur'an. Existing at the core of Mohamed's work, the verses offer the prospect of a bright future compared to the stark reality of destruction.

Every detail of Mohamed's work brings a part of Syria to life, from the miniature porcelain plates representing how neighbours would share food to the subtle decorations of buildings baring Greek and Roman symbols. "I feel it's my duty to be doing this work," says Mohamed. "It's not a privilege. It's not a luxury. It's a duty." There's a serene ambience to his studio, imbued with the smell of Syrian coffee and incense and the sound of Arabic music. But it's the artwork, not the studio, that the artist calls his "cocoon." For Mohamed, making art is therapy.

VIEW OF ARTIST'S STUDIO

FACADE
2013, 30 × 30 × 6 cm
Cast plaster, wood, rusted metal, fabric,
clay, found objects, pigment

WHY HAVE YOU
FORSAKEN US?!
2017, 91 × 152 × 30 cm
Mixed media, plaster, paint, rusted
metal, found objects

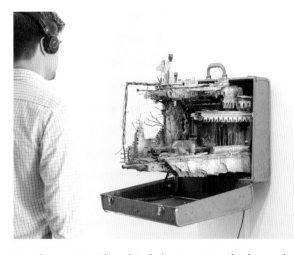

Mohamed's work reflects his deep interest in the cross-disciplinary exploration of street art and the realistic. The scenes he creates deliberately stand in stark contrast to the messages contained within them, such as audio recordings from his homeland. Qur'anic verses are presented as spray-painted acts of revolutionary protest or in the form of an audio loop from a hidden source intended to defy the dictatorial regimes of the region.

For the series *UNPACKED: Refugee Baggage*, Mohamed began placing his sculptures inside old suitcases. With Iraqi-born writer Ahmed Badr, he interviewed refugees from Afghanistan, Syria, the Democratic Republic of Congo, Iraq, and Sudan, gathering their thoughts about home. After each interview, Mohamed returned to his studio to model what he'd heard, capturing the memories of lost places. "People's lived experiences are shaped by their built environment," he says. "When you learn more about people you feared, you learn they're not that different from you. At the end of the day, there are thousands of architects who can build a shiny skyscraper, but how many can build a bridge between people in xenophobic times?"

The idea for *Desperate Cargo* came to Mohamed after an emotional visit to Europe. Mohamed's brother-in-law had been forced to leave Damascus to secure a better future for his sister and their children, making a terrifying journey across the Mediterranean in an inflatable craft and ending up in Sweden. It was hard for Mohamed to imagine his brother-in-law, a fellow architect, living in a camp with ninety other refugees from two dozen countries. Yet like so many displaced persons, these were

VISITOR EXPERIENCING THE ARTIST'S WORK AT THE EXHIBITION "UNPACKED: REFUGEE BAGGAGE"

CALL UPON ME . . .
2014, 38 × 38 × 17 cm
Mixed media, plaster, paint, rusted metal, found objects

FROM THE SERIES "DAMASCENE ATHAN"
2018, 86 × 61 × 20 cm
Mixed media, plaster, paint, rusted metal, found objects

not impoverished people with no education or aspirations; rather, they were ordinary citizens, with families and careers, who had been forced by conflict to flee their homes in search of a better life.

In January 2022, an exhibition of Mohamed's work, *What is Home to You?*, opened in Doha, Qatar. The question of the title runs throughout Mohamed's practice, from his sculpture to inspirational talks and projects in schools, opening up discussions about cultural diversity. In the artist's own words, "There is nothing like art to unite people in a divided society."

DESPERATE CARGO
2016, 365 × 120 × 100 cm
Mixed-media installation,
plaster, paint, float, found
objects, MP3 player, rusted
metal, lighting

75

JOSIE JENKINS

Josie Jenkins is an artist based in Liverpool. Her practice encompasses both the making of visual art and the organizing and execution of artistic projects. The box works shown here were made as a part of a collaboration to commemorate the centenary of the start of the First World War. The works were produced to accompany the one-night-only performance of a piece of music by British songwriters Bill Ryder-Jones, KOF, and John Herring, France's Moongaï, Russia's Noonwraith and Archngl, and the Manchester Camerata, specially commissioned for Liverpool International Music Festival 2014. The artists involved were asked to use the idea of "home" as a starting point. "For me," says Josie, "home is closely related to familiarity. *There Shall Be in that Rich Earth a Richer Dust Concealed* and *Washed by the Rivers, Blest by Suns of Home* use images from the landscape of the East Riding of Yorkshire, where I lived for the first part of my life and where my family still lives. Although this is my home, I like the idea that the physical layers that make up the artworks, together with the subject matter, create a sense of ambiguity, enough perhaps for anyone to be familiar with this place. The East Riding of Yorkshire is flat—it is not dramatic—but when you look into the boxes, something quite ordinary becomes special and alluring."

The boxes are made from pitch pine. Josie told her framer that she wanted to use some old wood for the boxes, but was finding it hard to describe what she was looking for. He showed her a piece of wood he'd taken from the back of an old picture frame, and it turned out to be precisely what she had envisaged. (The wood had come from a painting he was re-framing for another customer. When asked what he'd do if the customer wanted the old frame back, he said he'd tell them it had woodworm.) After asking around, Josie managed to source some more pitch pine from an old piece of furniture. She claims she enjoys using the wood because it too has a sense of familiarity; in the case of the boxes, she says, it gives each work the feeling of an old piece of furniture as well as an air of history. The titles of the boxes are taken from the famous First World War poem "The Soldier" by Rupert Brooke.

WASHED BY THE RIVERS,
BLEST BY SUNS OF HOME
2014, 29 × 38 × 8 cm
Graphite powder, ink, pencil on
paper and reclaimed pitch pine,
etched plastic, glass

THERE SHALL BE IN THAT
RICH EARTH A RICHER
DUST CONCEALED
2014, 38 × 40 × 8 cm
Graphite powder, ink, pencil on
paper and reclaimed pitch pine,
etched plastic, glass

SOPHIE SMALLHORN

Sophie Smallhorn's work explores the relationships between colour, volume, and proportion through a variety of mediums, including sculpture, print, and large-scale site-specific installations. Known for her strong use of colour, her biggest project to date is probably her involvement in the creation of the London Olympic Stadium. Sophie was commissioned by Populous Architects to put together a spectrum of colours for the stadium's exterior fabric "wrap" and internal features.

Sophie's commissions come from both corporate and private clients. "I made furniture at college," she explains, "and was definitely on the design path. But the sculptural pieces started to evolve, initially made from offcuts from the furniture projects. I certainly didn't set out to be an artist, but it's a very good place to be now.

"My mum was a textile designer so I was brought up with quite a lot of colour around, and ever since college my work has centred around colour. I like the endless possibilities of it and the idea that you can make a seemingly 'difficult' colour work within a piece. In fact, it's essential to work with the tricky colours, otherwise a composition can just be too safe."

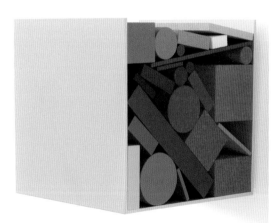

The works shown here demonstrate how interesting things can become when we allow for a bit of disarray.

COMPONENT CUBE 6
2016, 15 × 15 × 15 cm
Shelved fabricated materials, pigment

COMPONENT CUBE 5
2016, 15 × 15 × 15 cm
Shelved fabricated materials, pigment

CUBE 27/5
2015, 15 × 15 × 15 cm
Shelved fabricated materials, pigment

JAN VAN SCHAIK

"Years ago, while walking around the base of the Parthenon in Athens, I noticed, clearly discernible in its base, remnants of the great monument's former iterations, scarred by the battles that violently transformed them from architecture to rubble. So too, the blocks of these found Lego pieces bear the marks and discolouring left on them by their former owners before putting them up for sale on the second-hand market."

Jan van Schaik is an architect, researcher, and lecturer. His project *Lost Tablets* is a series of works that express the tension between a universally recognizable children's toy and the grammar of architectural symbols. Each of the works in the series has the same overall dimensions, a dynamic face, and a sheer face. The architecture of the sheer face is bound by the tension between the new profile of the tablet and the varying surface qualities of the found blocks, each with the markings of its own history. The architecture of the dynamic face is bound by the tension between an expectation of what a Lego composition would usually involve and the language of an imagined collective architectural unconscious. "The strange resonant familiarity of the tablets," explains Jan, "oscillates between the platonic, almost primal recognizability of Lego and the architectural grammar of the city caves of Matera, the churches of [Francesco] Borromini, the arches of the Doge's Palace in Venice, the buttresses of Gothic cathedrals, and the blue ceilings of the Shah Mosque of Isfahan." Each of these places, forms, or buildings carries with it a rich lineage combined with endless years of art appreciation. Jan believes that, in order to understand the great mysteries of the unknown, new languages need to be created.

Some of the works in the *Lost Tablets* series are named after ships that were found adrift with no sign of the crew, or which sunk in mysterious circumstances. Others are named after decommissioned satellites that now occupy "graveyard orbits" around the earth. The series' title comes from the whimsical idea that the Ten Commandments were in fact the Twenty Commandments—written on

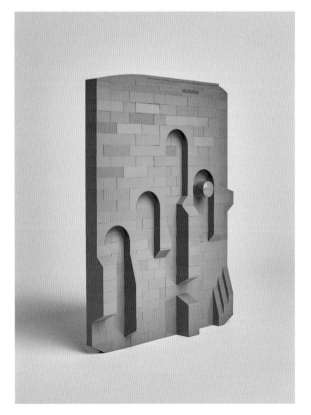

DEMETER
2021, 19 × 24.5 × 2.5 cm
Reconfigured Lego

Demeter *is named after a fictional ship in the 1897 novel* Dracula *by Bram Stoker. As depicted in the book, the* Demeter *was a Russian sailing vessel found drifting into harbour, the captain dead at the wheel, and a cargo of nothing but boxes of earth.*

ALOUETTE I
2021, 19 × 24.5 × 8.3 cm
Reconfigured Lego

Alouette I *is named after a Canadian satellite that studied the ionosphere. The satellite was deactivated in 1972, but is estimated to remain in orbit for the next thousand years.*

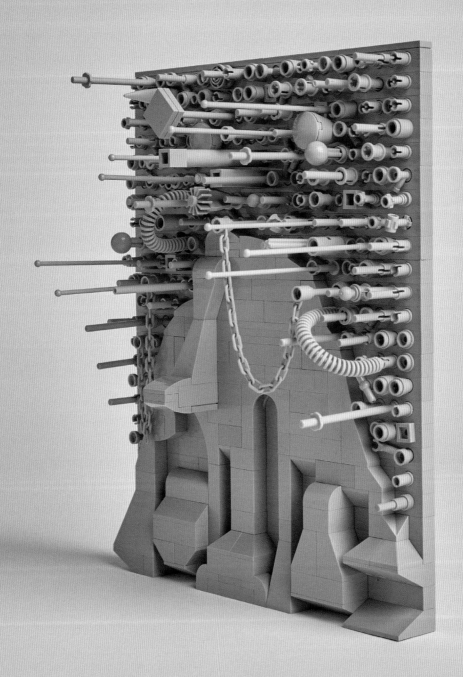

two tablets—and that Moses dropped one of the tablets on his way down from Mount Sinai. Jan likes the idea that the mysteries of the human condition are in fact the result of some missing instructions.

Jan is drawn to making these works, he says, as they are forms of pure architectural expression. Likewise, he is fascinated by the Lego blocks as a material because they are universally recognizable yet also neutral. There is nothing that cannot be made with Lego. This means that the ultimate form the pieces take has nothing to do with Lego at all. Yet the fact that they are Lego cannot be unseen. It is this conflict between the materiality of the objects and the meaning they have that appeals to the artist, and which enables the tablets to be both monuments of intangible meaning and immediately familiar. Jan says the last 5 per cent of making a work is often the part that takes the longest. In this final stage he begins to name the objects, a process that influences their final form. The tablets also have their own display options, such as steel shelves, wooden plinths, or sometimes a glass dome. According to Jan, "The mechanisms of display are an integral part of the works, as they invite you to see them the same way I do."

Opposite top
FLEETWING
2021, 19 × 24.5 × 4.8 cm
Reconfigured Lego

Fleetwing *takes its name from a schooner that mostly carried grain between Chicago and Buffalo. At dusk on 16 September 1888,* Fleetwing *departed Menominee, Michigan, with a load of lumber bound for Chicago. She ran aground en route and was abandoned shortly thereafter.*

Opposite bottom
BLENHEIM
2020, 19 × 24.5 × 6.2 cm
Reconfigured Lego

This work shares its name with a gunship last seen in 1807. Built to expand the capabilities of the Royal Navy ahead of the Seven Years' War with France, she was last seen flying signals of distress after leaving Madras. No further trace of either the ship or her 590-strong crew has ever been found.

Left
ISMAILIA
2021, 19 × 24.5 × 2 cm
Reconfigured Lego in glass dome

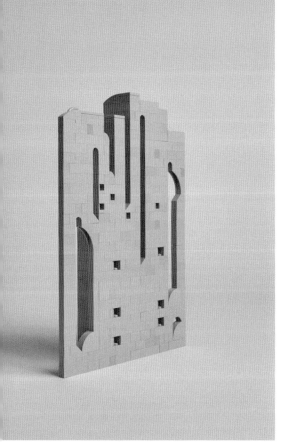

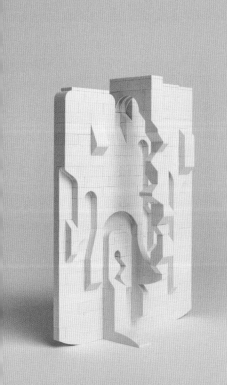

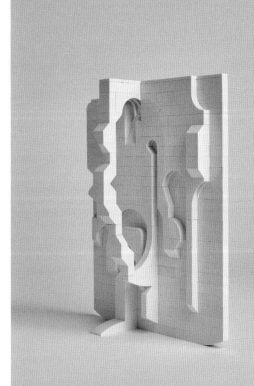

MARIA RIVANS

"Life, the universe, and everything" pretty much describes the content of Maria Rivans's surrealist worlds, where David Lynch meets Disney. Maria's three-dimensional collages turn fragments of vintage ephemera into fantastical landscapes and B-movie freeze-frames. Assembled from hundreds of cut-outs carefully culled from her huge collection of retro paraphernalia, they provide a true sensory overload. Influenced by Hitchcock and the golden age of Hollywood, Maria's works rewrite and reinvent screenplays of such classics as *Mildred Pierce* (1945), resulting in newly staged plots of the *Twilight Zone*. Fittingly, Maria's Brighton studio is a rather kooky building, purpose built as a small cinema in 1911.

Lurking in the Technicolor of each of her creations is a sense of urgency or danger. Also omnipresent are powerful leading ladies, such as Bette Davis and Joan Crawford, who made a huge impression on the young Maria. Other inspirations include such pin-ups as Hedy Lamarr, who is famous not only for being on the silver screen but also for being an inventor and pioneer in the field of wireless communications. This kind of detail is never diminished in Maria's storytelling. She is also a great fan of such artists as Eduardo Paolozzi and Hieronymus Bosch, as can be seen in the vibrant fauna of her *Pin-ups* series, inspired by Bosch's *The Garden of Earthly Delights*. In 2020, Maria's first book, *Extraordinary Things to Cut Out and Collage*, was published as the perfect remedy to lockdown.

GOODY YUM YUM
2013, 72.5 × 103 × 12 cm
Collaged paper and ephemera

THERE'S SOMETHING ABOUT MY OWN VOICE THAT FASCINATES ME
2019, 30 × 23 × 5.5 cm
Collaged paper and ephemera

Pages 86–87
ME TARZAN, YOU MAD MEN
2015, 61 × 86.5 × 12 cm
Collaged paper and ephemera

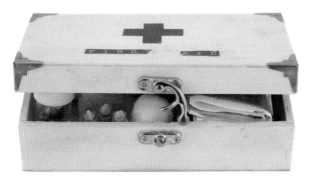

TRACEY WATKINS

Although she has always been interested in art, Tracey Watkins did not pursue a creative career, ending up working as a senior clerk for Lloyds Bank instead. Then, Tracey suffered a traumatic head injury, which resulted in a transient ischaemic attack (TIA), a temporary disruption of blood to the brain otherwise known as a "mini stroke." As well as causing her to lose her job, her head injury brought about a personality change; she could, she said, literally feel herself changing. Unlike in fiction, however, such as the story of Dr Jekyll and Mr Hyde, no one could *see* her changing. There was no murderous rage or hairy hands, just fear and crippling anxiety. Tracey thinks she cried every day for three years.

Bittersweet Symphony takes its title from a song by British rock band the Verve; it was also inspired by a line from the song's lyrics: "I'm a million different people from one day to the next." The concept behind the box is just that: the idea that people adopt different personalities in their everyday lives, especially those who have mental-health issues and need to take medication, either to bring out an acceptable persona or to suppress an unacceptable one. At the time of making the work, Tracey's personality was in a constant state of flux (she suffers from Bipolar 1 Disorder), and she was trying to medicate herself into a more stable condition. The irony is that, now she has attained a more stable mental state, her urge to make art has waned.

Tracey has lost many memories over the years, and often relies on others to remind her of things, people, and places. When she thinks about this loss, she says, her mind's eye conjures a swirling mass; she describes being sucked into a deep black vortex while hearing angry, gushing water. Tracey has since developed a strong urge to create physical "manifestations"—possibly, she thinks, to help her recreate lost memories. Once made, she has no interest in these manifestations and can happily give or throw them away. Their physicality has satisfied her need. The strange thing is, she says, that the memories she recreates may not be true, or might not have happened to her. She remembers falling off a bike and breaking her arm, for example, but has never been on a bicycle or broken a limb. But her sister has. This phenomena, of the brain finding a memory to fill a void and make it one's own, is called confabulation. At the time of writing, Tracey is involved in a project to make models for a doll's house. Like the act of making a memory, everything has to be in miniature.

BITTERSWEET SYMPHONY
(FIRST AID BOX)
2014, 22 × 10 × 8 cm
Mixed media in customized wooden box

E

A   R   **2**

                                          T

H

The work of Deepti Nair and Harikrishnan Panicker—a husband-and-wife artist duo based in Mumbai and known collectively as Hari & Deepti—is a cornucopia of ideas, all brought to life through their intricate illuminated paper-cut boxes and paper clay sculptures. They have, they say, always been drawn to the fantastical side of storytelling. Stories, especially fables, are often highly nuanced with hidden depths, making paper an ideal material with which to tell such stories and divine a greater meaning. As a material, it is minimal and intricate; it also interacts well with light, enabling the creation of limitless illusions.

Hari & Deepti started experimenting with paper-cut shadow boxes in 2010, cutting hand-painted watercolour paper and assembling it inside a wooden box to create a diorama. After years of working in this way, they started experimenting with lights, simplifying their pieces by losing the coloured aspect of the paper. This process led them to their own style of paper-cut art, incorporating backlit light boxes using flexible strips of LEDs. "What amazes us about the paper-cut light boxes," say the artists, "is the dichotomy of the piece in its lit and unlit state. The contrast is so stark that it has this mystical effect on the viewers."

The duo have travelled extensively in Asia and Europe, gathering ideas for stories and their craft, as well as showcasing work through solo shows and workshops. Their reputation has led to projects and commissions worldwide, including their debut book, *The Seekers*, a children's story based on a folk tale about of a group of brave adventurers who set out to save their village. The book was made using more than six hundred layers of paper and around twenty-five light boxes.

Page 91
THROUGH THE
WILDERNESS
2017, 50 × 40 × 26 cm
Hand-cut paper sculpture in
a light box

Opposite
NAUTILUS
2017, 78 × 78 × 32 cm
Hand-cut paper sculpture in
a light box

A commission inspired by
Jules Verne's classic novel
*Twenty Thousand Leagues
Under the Sea*, designed to look
like the view from the porthole
of Captain Nemo's submarine,
the *Nautilus*.

Top right
JOURNEY OF PAPER
Box installation 1 of 4
2018, 122 × 91 × 91 cm
Hand-cut paper sculpture in
a light box

This four-part installation was
created at the Pingtung Sugar
Factory in Taiwan as part of
a project designed to revive
the now-defunct paper mill,
which made paper from sugar-
cane waste, into a thriving
community arts space.

Bottom right
POOL OF RADIANCE
Pre-installation view

Overleaf
THE VALLEY OF KRUM
2019, edited scene from
The Seekers *(Knopf Books)*

"Paper is brutal in its simplicity as a medium.
It demands the attention of the artist while it
provides the softness they need to mould it
into something beautiful. It is playful, light,
colourless, yet magically colourful." *Hari & Deepti*

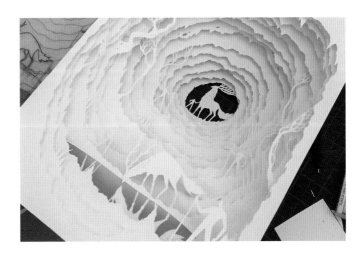

RYAN KAI

"I use place as a means of accessing something personal and relational. I often come back to a feeling of scale, or distance; how we fit into a much larger picture. I'm interested in how we, as individuals, relate to something as vast and nebulous as 'culture.'"

Ryan Kai is an exceptional contemporary painter. His approach is intuitive, often monochromatic, and he regularly incorporates sculptural elements to create something akin to a sensory installation. His aim, he says, is to make work that is as much "felt" as it is understood.

After studying fine art in Bristol, Ryan moved to London. During this transitional period in his life, he was actively involved in the grassroots street-art and graffiti scene on the south coast of England. He was also working internationally, creating murals as far away as Croatia and Athens as well as taking part in such art projects as *Transported* (2015), which used shipping containers to question ideas around global trade, consumption, and waste.

Drawing parallels between Ryan's practice then and now, there is still an evident interest in exploring both internal and external worlds. The works shown here speak to a time when he was trying out different techniques and materials, such as mould-making using silicone and resin. Ryan's insatiable appetite for new experiences is like that of a young man consumed by wanderlust; indeed, his involvement in the *Out of the Box* exhibitions captured an artist in transition, enthusiastically searching and experimenting.

BEARING
2014, 40 × 90 × 60 cm
Plaster block carried by terracotta people, scrim, pigment, steel

COPSE
2014, 30 × 50 × 12 cm
Assemblage in box, spruce pine, oil paint, glue

TECHO
2014, 20 × 30 × 12 cm
Assemblage, spruce pine, paper, balsa, aluminium, ink, drawing pin

CHRIS JENKINS

Born in the London borough of Greenwich in the late 1970s, Chris Jenkins has always been enthralled by the Thames—its rich maritime history and post-industrial landscape, the beaches of blackened bones from centuries of animal slaughter, the empty factories and boatyards. Many of these derelict moorings and warehouses are now gone, lost to the forces of gentrification and the endless building of riverside flats, blocking off the riverside walkways.

While the high-rises of Canary Wharf were taking shape on the opposite side of the river, Chris was busy in the bowels of condemned ships, saving relics and detritus far too interesting to be left to the mercy of the tide. Turning them into new forms became an obvious way to save and share them. This decision to re-use and repurpose was also a reaction to the escalating horror and madness of landfill. Chris is a stoic observer of how well things used to be made, compared to the inbuilt obsolescence of today's manufactured goods.

A fascination with the past, feeling it all around him rather than studying it in an academic sense, has led to Chris's current practice, creating forms that suggest and invite the viewer to perceive the greater narrative of which we are all a part. Such basic human needs as shelter and safety are explored through formations that appear ad hoc in nature but which have in fact been meticulously assembled. Central to Chris's practice is the idea of rebuilding through necessity rather than design—a primal roar in the face of time and decay.

In addition to his works made from found objects, Chris has created large public artworks, sculptures, installations, film and theatre sets, and immersive experiences. *The Cardboard Castle* is an ongoing, collaborative installation developed in partnership with artist Jo Hummel. For more than ten years, Chris and Jo have been erecting playful fortresses at high-profile festivals and art fairs. Made out of willow and roofing battens held together with a panelled cardboard canvas, the constructions have become sites of communal creative expression, especially among the young.

POPCORN
2015, 40 × 60 × 10 cm
Wood, paper, cellulose, found objects

THE SHIP
2017, 120 × 100 × 40 cm
Wood, wire, leather, found objects

POWER RIG
2016, 70 × 45 × 45 cm
Wood, wire, found objects, expanding foam

MATTHEW TUGWELL

According to one his friends, Matthew Tugwell is "a gentleman amateur enthusiast in many fields without a shred of finance." An online biography, meanwhile, claims that he "photographs and picks up stones"—a reference to his fascination with stone tools and his long-running interest in prehistory. Based in south London, Matthew is a photographer who spends a great deal of time making mischief with Photoshop. He also collects things: artefacts from the foreshore, maps, fossils, and other objects that take up space. Some things, he says, are made into other things and are photographed.

During lockdown, Matthew devoted much of his time to creating miniature scenes inside boxes. He also has a tradition of making his own, curious Christmas cards, and one year the subject was a tiny diorama under a glass dome that depicted the German photographers Bernd and Hiller Becher taking a photograph of a water tower. Having produced the diorama in Photoshop, Matthew decided to start making such things for real, taking inspiration from a number of different sources. One was a still from *The Signalman*, a short film from 1976 starring Denholm Elliott and based on an 1866 short story by Charles Dickens. Elliott plays the eponymous signalman, who is haunted by a vision at the mouth of a railway tunnel. Matthew's work, also called *The Signalman*, is a faithful recreation of the scene from the film over which the opening credits are played. It is also part of a ongoing series called *The Films of Denholm Elliott in Miniature*. Another of Matthew's ongoing projects, *Dolls House Vacancies*, suggests the endless melancholy of empty rooms. These lovingly found/manipulated/repurposed/edited interior spaces raise numerous questions: has someone just moved out, or is a forensics team about to walk in? The works recall the "Nutshell Studies of Unexplained Death," a series of intricately designed, doll house–styled dioramas created by Frances Glessner Lee, a pioneer of forensic science. Made in the first half of the twentieth century and based on real-life crimes, the models were used in lectures on the subject of crime-scene investigation.

THE SIGNALMAN
From the series The Films of Denholm Elliott in Miniature
2021, 45 × 29 × 44 cm
Scale ratio 1:76.2
Acrylic, sawdust, gypsum, glue, wire, leaves, wood, foam, lichen, moss, stone, plastic, Christmas lights

SELECTION OF WORKS FROM THE SERIES *DOLLS HOUSE VACANCIES*

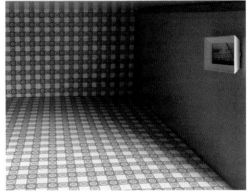

GALE ROTHSTEIN

Gale Rothstein's art has always been about "putting together the pieces." Her recent works include assemblages in which boxes and environments ("inter-exteriors") exist within a strong narrative and historical framework. Gale's practice is informed by her former career as a jewellery designer and life-long interest in antiques, collectibles, found objects, harvested broken appliances, and other used items. These she re-contextualizes and juxtaposes to create contrasting and surreal environments, prompting us to ask, "Where are we? Who is here with us? How big or small are we? Are we awake or dreaming?" Her aim is for the viewer to question their sense of time and place.

Gale's work is influenced by the memory of her father, who was a jack of all trades and one of the original recyclers and repurposers, decades before it was commonplace. Gale inherited her father's collection of spare parts and incorporates many of them into her assemblages, further strengthening the works' historical and personal foundations. Gale lives and works in the Greenwich Village neighbourhood of New York City.

A FACSIMILE OF WHAT
WE IMAGINED
2019, 56 × 76 × 33 cm
Mixed-media assemblage

GLENN ANDERSON

Glenn Anderson was born in Birmingham, England, in 1977. Growing up in a mixed-heritage (English/Welsh/Irish/Jamaican), working-class family, times were tough but colourful. His Irish grandmother would entertain Glenn and his cousins with late-night tales about the banshees, accompanied by either a cup of tea or a Guinness. There were stories from his father and uncles as well, about his Jamaican grandfather's superstitions. When his grandfather opened a telegram from his father (Glenn's great-grandfather), he would light a fire, open the letter, and pass it through the flames to cleanse it of any wrongdoing. Or he would make sure that a mirror faced his bedroom door, so that the duppy (a restless ghost in Jamaican culture) would see its own image and disappear. Glenn believes such stories, combined with the icons and trinkets of a Catholic upbringing, gave rise to his fascination with the supernatural.

Looking back at his youth in Newtown, an inner-city area of Birmingham, Glenn realizes how informative those years were, playing "Stig of the Dump" in a concrete jungle, with buddleia and butterflies popping up among the industrial waste and waterways. Glenn grew up surrounded by

different races, nationalities, and "refugees"—good people crushed by the unemployment of the Thatcher years. He witnessed families barely managing to function and all manner of mental-health issues. His own life at that time was relatively simple: a naive dreamer observing, interacting, and questioning; long summers with no money; fond memories of a loving family. Among Glenn's possessions is a crudely built box full of things, strange and magical objects that he has collected over time, the products of "loft and cupboard mooching." Whether good or bad, everything feeds into his art; indeed, perhaps its creation runs parallel to the piecing together of his own life story.

SELF-PORTRAIT
2012, 96 × 50 × 35 cm
Scrap wood, mixed-media
assemblage, paint

In 1990 Glenn's family moved to Gibraltar for two years, living on an old wooden sailing boat in Sheppard's Marina. This once-colourful marina has now been redeveloped, but it provided Glenn with a fast-track initiation into puberty and manhood. As the gateway to the Mediterranean, Gibraltar was full of adventure and intriguing characters from around the world, pirates included. It was a boys' paradise, with endless places to explore, from the Moorish Castle and the ancient tunnels going deep underground to the decommissioned bunkers and old medical barracks.

The sights, sounds and smells of Gibraltar, from the towering cliffs and scented flowers to the macaque monkeys, have never left Glenn; neither has an awareness that something much greater beckoned, just like Africa across the water. Arriving back in England proved quite a shock: rudderless, he quickly realized how bleak life could be. Aged fifteen, Glenn nearly died after being hit by a car, losing part of his right ear and gaining thirty-eight stitches and a hairline fracture to the skull.

The 1990s were a heady and challenging time for Glenn: magic mushrooms in the classroom, Jungle music and raves (it was also when he met the future mother of his twin daughters). Feeling as though his life was unravelling around him, he discovered the significance and focus of his art and, with a little help from his teachers, applied to study at De Montfort University in Leicester. This period in his life proved transformative, revealing to Glenn that creative practice is therapy. Meeting like-minded souls, he travelled to many different countries, working commercially on numerous art projects, from humble school workshops to exhibitions. Glenn became fascinated with nature, culture, architecture, people, makers, music and food – an exotic fusion of skills and crafts, all consciously and unconsciously rebuilding and reshaping his work.

Above
SHAMBALA DRAGON BURN
2011

Opposite (details left)
THE BOX OF DELIGHTS
2010–, 90 × 90 × 24 cm
Assorted junk, mixed media,
paint

Around 2009 a natural shift occurred in Glenn's practice. Leaving behind his sketchy, two-dimensional, mixed-media work, he moved towards creating three-dimensional sculptural figurines and arrangements. The following year he single-handedly built his first "burn" for the Shambala Festival in Northamptonshire. Although it was not his best work, the process of making it ignited a creative spark, giving him an insight into the power of ritual and of incorporating the sacred element of fire with the techniques of ancient, inherited knowledge. Glenn has never had much in the way of financial backing or the help of assistants, yet he has enjoyed such cultural exchanges in locations as far afield as São Paulo, Amsterdam and Galicia.

Glenn has also made some extraordinary pieces for use on stage, working with the likes of Swedish band GOAT. These totem effigies are often lit as the finale to such events as Lunar Festival, including on one occasion by legendary "Fire" singer Arthur Brown. Collaboration is of great importance to Glenn, who has worked with a wide range of organizations and individuals, from Cirque du Soleil and Greenpeace to Lucy McLauchlan and Gent 48, to name but a few. Other notable life events include exhibiting at Lab 101 Gallery in Culver City, California, and a chance encounter with Hollywood actor Dennis Hopper, which resulted in Glenn and three fellow Brummies receiving a personal tour of Hopper's photography exhibition.

These days, Glenn is devoting more time to family, learning, and "renovation"—both personal and professional. He has also discovered that life begins at forty: a second chance, fatherhood, seeing the world through the eyes of his four-year-old son. Life, says Glenn—its memories and symbols, landmarks of change and meaning—feeds his art.

This page
The artist's Bird Holding a Cube *(centre)*
before and after being lit by a member of Sun
Ra Arkestra (top) at the 2015 Lunar Festival.

Opposite
THE GUARDIAN
2012, 100 × 40 × 32 cm
Mixed-media assemblage, paint
Inspired by a collection of stones and
Paulo Coelho's The Alchemist

JULIE LIGER-BELAIR
IN THE ROOMS OF MY MIND

reflected dream.   julie liger belair 2020

Julie Liger-Belair is a collector at heart, constantly gathering fragments of ideas and objects, each with their own story to tell. She grew up in an artistic household surrounded by art books and art supplies, spending her summers in the Canadian wilderness, absorbing and observing, letting her imagination run away with nature. After studying music and visual arts, she honed her practice at Ontario College of Art and Design, taking classes in printmaking, photography, illustration, and metal-smithing. The fusion of these skills led her towards mixed-media art—an attempt to combine different disciplines in one coherent body of work.

Around this time, Julie began collecting cabinet cards and Victorian-era photographs, the "seeds" of her very distinctive work. For more than twenty years now, she has been making assemblages and three-dimensional collages in readymade or handmade frames and boxes, using paint, wood, papier-mâché, polymer clay, metal, and found objects. The inclusion of cabinet photos imbues the assemblages with a "life force," evoking imagined histories and feelings of nostalgia. The stern nature of these portraits provides an effective contrast to the works' humour and levity.

Julie's pieces are clearly playful, featuring all kinds of iconography—altar pieces for everyday life, making sacred of the mundane. Her more recent work attempts to combine these vernaculars, the ironic and the sacred, to tell a story about the disconnect between our private and public selves. Who we are is often at odds with what we project to others, and Julie's work questions what it is that we choose to reveal, conceal, or fabricate. More importantly, it explores the toll exacted by this "duplicity": specifically, the feelings of sorrow, resentment, anxiety, and martyrdom it engenders.

Above
REFLECTED DREAM
2020, 32 × 24 cm
Mixed-media collage

Left
Detail of the artist's contribution to
Strike a Light, *a matchbox project*
organized by Edinburgh Collage
Collective, 2020

Opposite
LOST WITH THE DOLLS
2016, 40.6 × 30.5 × 9 cm
Mixed-media assemblage and
found objects

Julie also has a love of houses. "The simple little image of a triangle on top of a square that all kids learn to draw early on, and most every one around the world recognizes as a symbol for 'dwelling' and 'home,' is so evocative and stimulates my imagination in so many ways. The house can symbolize the place where we are most comfortable, most ourselves, a place of warmth and protection. But it can just as easily symbolize a place where we feel trapped or where bad things can happen out of the public eye. The house can symbolize our inner world, the windows being our eyes that can look both in or out, that can divulge the inner turmoil or, on the contrary, keep it well hidden behind drawn curtains. For this reason I love drawing houses with no doors, forbidding entry or exit and only windows to see in or out of, a both comforting and scary notion." In a recent series, Julie chose to paint over existing paintings. "I love the act of recycling older work," she explains, "allowing some of the images to show through and so starting a conversation, if you will, between the new ideas and older ideas."

Reflecting on the strangeness of the last few years, Julie says that Instagram proved an invaluable tool during lockdown, which she shared with three small children and a dog. For someone not keen on social media, it not only allowed her to make a living but also connected her with such like-minded international artists as Rhed Fawell. Out of such online encounters came *Februllage*, a joint collaboration between Edinburgh Collage Collective and the Scandinavian Collage Museum inviting collage artists to make a "collage a day" throughout the month of February using the Februllage Official Word Prompt. If you are perpetual thinker like Julie, such projects are heaven-sent. In the manner of fairy tales and dreams, her surreal worlds help make sense of our surroundings and explain our fears.

Below
LITTLE PAPER HOUSE
2019, mixed-media maquette experiment

Opposite
LANGUAGE OF OBJECTS
2020, assortment of Frebullage and pandemic sketchbook spreads

Pages 112–113
THE FLIGHTLESS BIRDS
2018, 76.2 × 101.6 × 5 cm
Collage and painting on cradled birch board

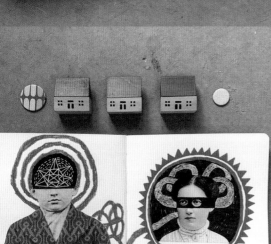

MAHA AHMED

Maha Ahmed is a Pakistani artist best known for her small-scale, intricate paintings that explore otherworldly visions of fantastical creatures and distant worlds. These places are as beautiful as they are potentially frightening, drawing on feelings of isolation and wonder, depicting the experience of identity and belonging in the great unknown.

The exquisite miniature assemblages shown here were included in the first *Out of the Box* exhibition. *Red Shoes*, for example, is the story of a girl in the 1950s who was taken to a small shop in Lahore to buy black shoes for school; instead, a beautiful pair of red shoes caught her eye. She pleaded and begged her mother to buy them for her, and still remembers the day she wore those perfect little red shoes to school. Now, however, this once confident young girl is unrecognizable, broken by an unhappy marriage. "I felt as though she had to box herself up," observes Maha, "hide herself so far deep somewhere that she lost herself along the way."

Maha's interest in boxes, she says, can be traced back to her childhood. "My mother had a kumiko box—a Japanese wooden inlay box made of different coloured wood intricately joined together to create a scenery. It may have been Mount Fuji but I can't be sure. It was something she adored and would place her valuables in. I remember running my finger over the inlay to feel the unevenness of the wood and trace it with my fingertips. It was so simple yet so beautiful. It was purposefully placed on my mother's dressing table until, one day, the lid disappeared. She still kept that box for years to come but the jewels and trinkets were replaced by nail cutters, buttons, tweezers, and reels of thread that she would find lying around the house and it was moved where it was needed. The repurposing of this box along with the memory of what it once was stayed with me throughout my life." Maha presently lives and works in Dubai. She says she still collects beautiful boxes, but they are all empty.

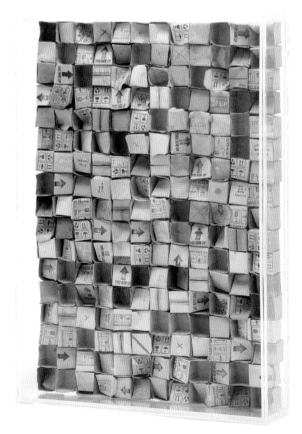

BOXED UP
2014, 42 × 29 × 6 cm
1 of 3 parts
Photo transfers on coffee-stained
handmade paper boxes

RED SHOES
2012, 38.5 × 25.5 × 5 cm
Photo transfers on coffee-stained
handmade paper boxes

CLEMENS GRITL

Born in Germany, Clemens Gritl is a visionary artist who digitally crafts two- and three-dimensional models for his series *A Future City from the Past*—a reflective exploration of twentieth-century urban utopias.

Like J. G. Ballard's dystopian novel *High-Rise*, Clemens is interested in the question of whether modern architecture can affect people's behaviour. Can a residential tower truly create social tension, aggression, and anarchy? Clemens's particular focus is the interaction between the spaces, dimensions, monotony, and materiality of urban megastructures. He is fascinated by the optimism of the post-war era; with how a prefabricated, futuristic metropolis might age; and by the kind of atmosphere that a man-made landscape, constructed of only concrete and asphalt, would generate.

Clemens's project is informed by the notion of *Wohnmaschinen* (living machines), architectural behemoths encompassed by endless motorway networks. With an appreciation for the work of the English architect Rodney Gordon, Clemens is also captivated by Brutalism and an architectural age of unforced, positive thinking. He supports the ideals of a compact, vertical city, but acknowledges that many mistakes were made in the past, such as the lack of infrastructure, public transport, leisure opportunities, and maintenance that led to the inevitable decay of many projects.

All of Clemens's artworks are informed by his wide-ranging knowledge of architects and architectural movements, from Japanese Metabolism and Le Corbusier to the New Topographic Movement. He is also profoundly influenced by the cityscape photography of Lewis Baltz, who, like Clemens, captures silent environments without motion or people, where nothing can distract the viewer from surfaces, objects, and the buildings themselves.

N O # 0 6
2020, 145 × 220 cm
Architectural computer model printed on Hahnemühle Photo Rag Baryta

N O # 0 4
2017, 220 × 130 cm
Architectural computer model printed on Hahnemühle Photo Rag Baryta

NO#08
2020, 90 × 160 cm
Architectural computer
model printed on Hahnemühle
Photo Rag Baryta

LINDA HUBBARD

Whether you interpret Pandora's box as a prison or a pantry, life is not hopeless; rather, human beings are hopelessly human. Linda Hubbard is somebody who cares. She asks you to look inside yourself and think. She also tells it as it is: "I sculpt, paint, and draw; this is what I do. I try hard. I went to art college. I have exhibited in empty shops. On the streets of our world. In big art houses. Rich nobby folk have bought my work. Not so rich folk have also bought my work. Folks who have turned to the dark side have tried to buy my work. I have given work away. You may have seen my work in the *Big Issue*. You may have seen my work in 'shiny shiny' books. You can always see my work on the web for free. I want to contribute. I strive to make a difference. Protest. Resist."

Left
HISTORY & CHIPS
From the project Family Snaps
Relined vintage box, chip made of plaster, oil paint

Below
OUT OF DATE
OCCUPATION DATES
From the project Not in My Fridge
"Inedible. These glistening jewels of apartheid are painted bronze."

Opposite top
EMPIRE WINDRUSH
Photograph, wooden black emoji

Opposite bottom left
TAKING BACK CONTROL OF OUR BORDERS
"Roundup weedkiller, the final solution. Comes with miniature rubber gloves and a miniature lasso. Everything you need to eliminate those weeds from your borders."

Opposite bottom right
RELIQUARY
From the project Suggestivism
"Efes Toasted Burger Muffin Donald Trump Apparition"

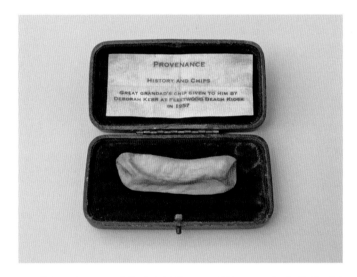

GUY TARRANT

"While working in different schools, I became interested in the collections of confiscated objects I came across in teachers' desk drawers. I began to talk to staff about these items and very quickly this turned into a kind of social research project."

Guy Tarrant's *The Confiscation Cabinets* consists of a collection of confiscated items gleaned from 150 London schools, articles withheld by teachers that were never claimed back. The contents of the cabinets, from pea-shooter pens and colourful plastic toys to jewellery and improvised weapons, reveal much about their original owners. Each tells its own particular story, such as the bag of chips made from paper by a girl with an eating disorder. One teacher seized a tennis ball containing 200 match heads, designed to ignite on impact. Taken as a whole, the cabinets represent the flotsam and jetsam of school life, as well as highlighting social difficulties and behavioural divisions around age, gender, and culture. The series has been shown at various venues around the UK, and is now part of the permanent collection of the V&A Museum of Childhood in London.

Guy has been making artworks since 1987. His projects are always reflexive in their approach; that is, they always seek to reflect issues pertaining to the situations he finds himself in. In addition, his artworks have always sought to challenge the formal processes of art; indeed, his early projects were concerned with questioning the very nature of artistic authorship and professional practice. Over time, Guy has become more involved in teaching, shifting his attention to addressing the education process itself. He has been involved in education for almost thirty years, and is dedicated to trying to improve the wider system. He is currently the lead teacher at a small, multi-site SEMH (social, emotional, and mental health) school, and continues to be involved in community arts projects, focusing specifically on mental-health issues.

DIET CHIPS
*Year 8 Girls
(Eaten to aid
weight loss)
1984, Outer London*

THE CONFISCATION
CABINETS
*Installation view (2 of 8
cabinets) at the V&A Museum of
Childhood*

A selection of confiscated items, Years 6 to 10
From "Resistance," a feature for issue 3 of The Quarterly
Photographs by Tom Brannigan

STEPHEN WRIGHT

For more than thirty years, Stephen Wright worked as an artist and designer, producing textiles, fashion collections, one-off fabrics, and even his own line of stationery. Increasingly disillusioned with the commercial design world, he was captivated by a 1998 BBC documentary presented by Jarvis Cocker called *Journeys Into the Outside*.

He and his partner, Donald, were so inspired by their discovery of outsider art that they decided to travel to France to see the work of Raymond Isidore and Bodan Litnianski. The extraordinary creations of these "naive architects" moved Stephen to transform his suburban Victorian home in south London into the "House of Dreams." Slowly but surely, he turned the ground floor and garden of the house into a complete artistic environment, decorated with large-scale mosaics, constructions of papier mâché and cement, and compositions made up of such found objects as false teeth, broken dolls, bottle tops, and wigs. This fantastical creation is interwoven with handwritten memory boards recalling significant events in Stephen's life. "We wanted to make something that we were going to leave behind," he explains. "Little did I know that Donald and my parents would pass away only a few years later. A lot of my angst went into the House of Dreams; it was therapy."

There are numerous moving stories tucked among the magical medley of endless things, paintings, records, old photographs, and flea-market gems that populate the house. This carefully curated home is a sanctuary of love and loss, a memorial to thousands of ordinary, sometimes forgotten lives. "Everything in this house is here for a reason," says Stephen. "Nearly everything's from other countries, from Haiti, South America, Brussels, and a lot from Paris. I do all the junk markets, buy all the crap and make something out of it. You only live once; if it speaks to me, I buy it."

Stephen's strong work ethic can be traced back to his childhood, growing up in a humble, eighteenth-century cottage in rural Cheshire. His father was also an avid collector who would "find things on the road." Stephen has bequeathed the House of Dreams to the National Trust, and for the last eight years it has been open to the public as a museum, with lively tours provided by Stephen himself and his new partner, Michael. "The house is quite demanding; I have a love–hate relationship with it," confesses Stephen, who sometimes fantasizes about packing his bags and leaving the place for good in the manner of Simon Rodia, the sole creator of the legendary Watts Towers in Los Angeles.

I MISS THOSE DAYS
2014, 45.5 × 25 × 12 cm
Mixed media, foil, paint, and plastic

MY ANGEL MACHOOCHOO
2015, 101 × 140 × 20 cm
Stitched fabric and paint

I'M YOUR PUPPETEER
2010, 100 × 122 × 15 cm
Stitched fabric and paint

FRANK JENNINGS
DECEPTIVE RECEPTACLES

"Aged about ten, I was sitting on a canal bank watching my friends swimming. I arbitrarily pressed my forefinger and thumb into the soil where my hand rested, squeezing them together. I was rather shocked to discover that they did not meet as expected. Pulling my fingers out through the soil, I found that I was rich beyond my wildest dreams: I was holding a six penny piece."

This was the first of several random events that have occurred throughout Frank Jennings's life. The strangest of them all, he says, happened in the early 1980s, when he saw two men walk into each another, both blind, and neither aware of what had actually happened. The phenomenon of chance plays a major role in Frank's art. Over the years, he has amassed a plethora of objects and artefacts that he regards as potential material for his work: it has been his practice to display such items in close proximity to one another, enabling them to foster a relationship. As Joseph Cornell once said, "Who knows what one object will tell another?" Occasionally, Frank will use a person—either real or fictitious—as a starting point. Such individuals as Brunel, Columbus, Houdini, and Don Quixote have all made appearances in his work. The seashell made its debut some twenty-five years ago, initially as a single component, then progressing into multiple usages in the series *Hermit Crab Museums*. With each work in the series, Frank has endeavoured not to duplicate a single "species." The object placed inside each shell is determined both by the shell's appearance and by Frank's interpretation of its shape, such as cave, kennel, kiosk, pram, and goalmouth.

THE BOYHOOD OF BRUNEL
1982, 47 × 42 × 13 cm
Metal, driftwood, chain, wood, glass

SURREALIST HERMIT CRAB
MUSEUM
2013, 50.5 × 41 × 10 cm
Shells, miscellaneous objects,
wood, glass

In 1973, having originally trained as a mechanical engineer, Frank enrolled at Leeds Polytechnic to study fine art. It was in Leeds that he established a preference for object-making, moving on from his initial interest in painting. As he explored this art form in more detail, he became convinced that the assemblage/box format was the perfect vehicle for combining a number of long-standing interests: museums, collecting miscellanea, and his encounters with the phenomenon of chance. He is keen to stress, however, that it is his own conscious intervention and manipulation of the disparate that is central to the creation of his work, and not simply the "chance encounter" that the surrealists embraced.

On the subject of the surrealists, Frank shares his birthday with René Magritte, a coincidence about which he is particularly delighted. He also happens to own a telephone that Magritte once possessed. What's more, among his books is a copy of the pulp-fiction novel *Les Émeraudes Sanglantes* by Raoul Whitfield that bears Magritte's signature; this, Frank predicts, will be gloriously incorporated into a future box.

Frank has always been interested in the origins of assemblage, and likes to think of *Little Dancer Aged Fourteen*, a sculpture completed by Edgar Degas in 1881, as an early example. Degas used several of his paintbrushes to construct the armature for the original wax figure and then tied her wax ponytail with a real silk ribbon and dressed her in a gauze tutu—an early instance of an artist using an object to represent itself. Eventually, thirty or so bronze statues were cast from the original wax figure, each of which is unique owing to the care, or lack of it, given to its accruements. Exactly one hundred years after this pioneering sculpture, Frank notes that the American artist Jasper Johns used several paintbrushes propped up in a coffee tin as the subject for a series of bronzes.

RETREAT, RETREAT
2014, 20 × 12 × 5 cm
Driftwood, sea shells, string, wood, glass

COLUMBUS'S CARDIGAN
1994, 50 × 46 × 11.5 cm
Wool, paper, knitting needles, wood, glass

A SHELL OF HER FORMER SELF
2010, 29 × 31.5 × 12.5 cm
Nautilus shell, mother-of-pearl buttons, wood, glass

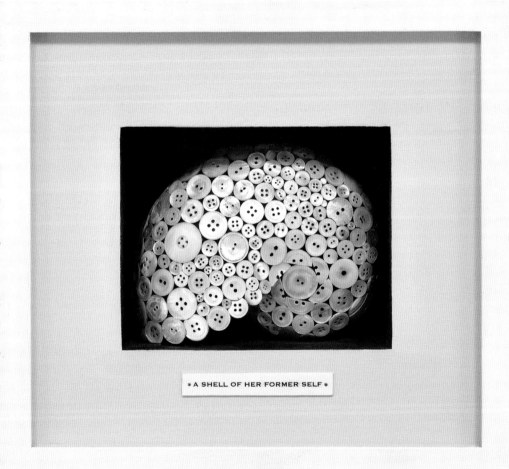

* A SHELL OF HER FORMER SELF *

"As beautiful as the chance encounter of a sewing machine and an umbrella on an operating table." *Comte de Lautréamont*

Reading the poetic novel *Les Chants de Maldoror*, French surrealist André Breton discovered this singular phrase that became foundational to the surrealist doctrine of objective chance.

No doubt owing to his engineering background, Frank's works are immaculately constructed. In terms of craftsmanship, zaniness, and humour, he believes his work has more in common with that of the American sculptor H. C. Westermann than with the more worn and lived-in quality and enigmatic feel of a Joseph Cornell box. Frank's aim is to retain the original identity of the objects he uses, placing his "manipulated marriages" in display cases built by his own hand. The box format, notes Frank, not only harmonizes the disparateness of the contents but also elevates them to the status of something precious. His titles, which are both cryptic and witty, are carefully considered to provide an insight into the individual works.

In 1983, after teaching art part-time in Bradford and Leeds, Frank secured a permanent post in the art department at South Downs College, Hampshire, where he thrived until his retirement as head of art in 2008. Frank's studio is located next to his eighteenth-century cottage and the River Rother in the sleepy village of Sheet, near Petersfield, also in Hampshire. He continues to make his "deceptive receptacles" from this idyll, extensively collecting and exhibiting.

THE NIGHT THE MIDNIGHT
MILK RACE TURNED SOUR
2003, 25 × 29 × 10 cm
Emery paper, graphite paste,
model figures, wood, glass

SLO MO
2013, 22 × 51 × 8.5 cm
Resin figure, pearl necklace, felt,
wood, glass

THE CHANCE ENCOUNTER
OF A COWBOY AND A
SEWING MACHINE ON THE
CORNER OF MY KITCHEN
TABLE
2002, 36 × 18 × 18 cm
Model cowboy, toy sewing
machine, wood, glass, fabric

131

CHRIS HAWKINS

It is his training and experience as a goldsmith, says Chris Hawkins, that has helped him refine his interest in the miniature. The tactile nature of handheld objects forms a common thread in his work, linking both his jewellery and his small sculptural works. Most of his jewellery is initially sculpted in wax before being cast in metal using the lost wax process. Chris's inspirations include the artisans of the Edo period in Japan and the metalwork of the Renaissance, as well as nature and history more generally.

Before the invention of photography, lovers would often exchange tokens of devotion and affection, a box or locket containing a representation of themselves—a lock of hair or a small likeness. Sometimes it would just be a painting of one of the lover's eyes. *Lips* is Chris's interpretation of these long-abandoned symbols of endearment, housed in an old jewellery box that emphasizes the "taboo" nature of its contents and enables them to be kept secret.

Another of Chris's interests—the imagery and symbolism associated with reliquaries—came about during a visit to Saint Mark's Basilica in Venice, where he saw the finger bone of an unknown saint displayed under glass. Chris describes *The Owl Reliquary* as an amalgamation of ideas around preservation and decay, evoking both the mundane and the profound. The "owl" of the work is made from the tide-worn bowl of a Victorian clay pipe, an object that is commonly found on the banks of the Thames. Something about its shape and patina suggested the body and ghostly plumage of a barn owl, a bird steeped in mythology and magic.

LIPS
2014, 4 × 2.5 × 1.8 cm
Painted polymer clay
in antique jewellery
presentation box

THE OWL
RELIQUARY
2018, 6.5 × 6.5 × 7 cm
Salvaged Victorian
pipe bowl, painted and
gilded rodent bones
in adapted 19th-
century Italian glass
souvenir box

STEFFEN DAM

Originally trained as a toolmaker, Steffen Dam has been working with glass for twenty-five years. He began by blowing glass, but over the years has incorporated techniques borrowed from other crafts, such as casting and grinding. In the mistakes and faults he encountered—the unwanted air bubbles, ash marks, soot, cracks, and crookedness—Steffen found something that could not be predicted or sketched beforehand. Setting the established and traditional techniques aside, he started making glass all "wrong" in an attempt to capture the good in the bad. Out of these experiments came his fictional fossils, plants, and other objects, like frozen extracts of chaos to be watched undisturbed. Steffen's suspended little creatures remind us of how we read and feel both time and change.

"My aim," says Steffen, "is to describe the world as I see it. One could also say to describe what's not tangible and understandable with our everyday senses. My cylinders contain nothing that exists in the ocean, my specimens are plausible but not from this world, my plants are only to be found in my compost heap, and my flowers are still unnamed."

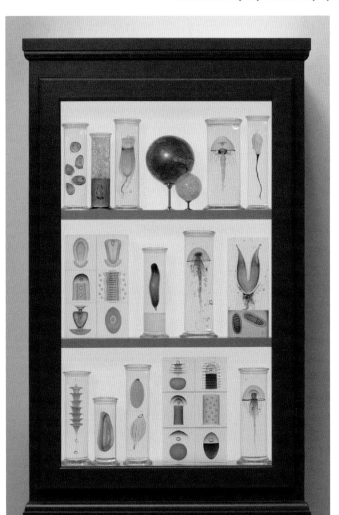

Left
CABINET OF CURIOSITIES
2013, 102 × 62 × 24 cm
Cabinet with fictitious specimens of flora and fauna, blown and cast glass backlit with dimmable light, 100-year-old pinewood cabinet

Opposite
THE OWL OF MINERVA TAKES FLIGHT IN THE DUSK
2015, 109 × 96.5 × 20 cm
Glass, metal, taxidermy, wood

Pages 136–137
MARINE LIFE JARS
2016, height 10–30 cm
Blown and cast glass

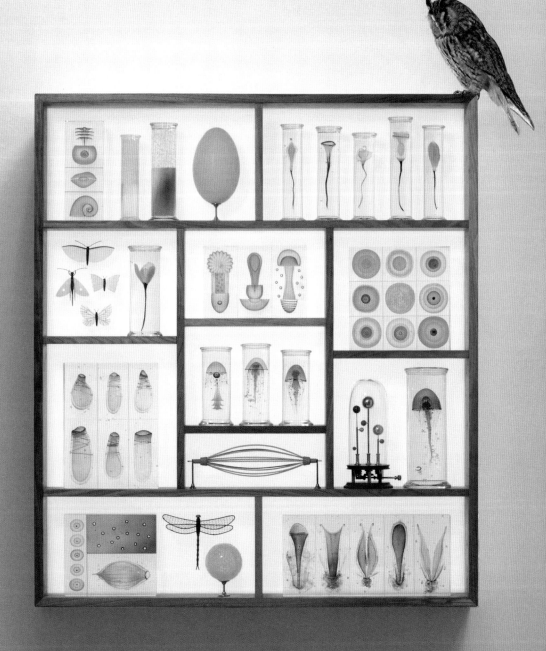

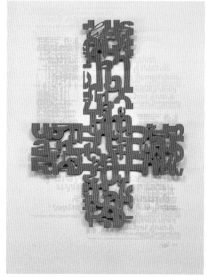

EMMA LLOYD

"So many people were shut up tight inside themselves like boxes, yet they would open up, unfolding quite wonderfully, if only you were interested in them." *Sylvia Plath*

Emma Lloyd's practice is concerned with some of the fundamental issues of human existence. What is it, for example, that roots us to our culture and ideologies? She is particularly interested in exploring the parameters within which we think and act, assessing the roles that language, experience, and environment play in the development of our world views.

In pursuing these issues, Emma began to explore her own Welsh heritage. Taking inspiration from Sylvia Plath's short story "Initiation," she decided to play with the structure of a box in order to represent the self, or the various aspects of self, a person might hold within them. This idea of fragmentation culminated in *Betabet*, which brought together a collection of boxes via a compositor's type case. Using the Welsh alphabet, Emma chose to explore a series of questions around the experience of learning to read, something that every child must go through. What if letters were still familiar but could not be read? How do they make us feel? Is the experience of uncertainty different as an adult? Is it more or less intimidating? Is it possible there are aspects of our history and culture we are unable to access because of language limitations? How much has our language informed who we are and who we will become?

Materials and their associations are as important to Emma's work as the concepts behind it. They should, Emma believes, enhance comprehension and reflect her ideas, connecting with a viewer's sense memories and prior experiences. Her work explores our very perception of matter.

TAMEIDIAU OHONA' I
2013, 53 × 35 × 10 cm
Sculpted double-sided screen print (edition of 8)

BETABET
2014, 82.3 × 36.4 × 41 cm
Sculpted full-colour atlas and compositor's case

STEVE TALBOT

"Working in collage and with these materials is an act of remembering. How we remember the past determines the way we inhabit the present."

Steve Talbot originally trained as a set designer, bringing a unique creative approach to BBC film and television productions, including the children's arts programme *Hartbeat* featuring the animated character Morph. A career change with a return to study led to a new role working in museums and galleries. He has, however, always been fascinated by boxes. As a child, Steve remembers receiving toys—cowboys and Indians, model trains, aeroplanes—in boxes with plastic windows displaying the treasures inside. It is, perhaps, this very particular display aesthetic that has provided the springboard for his practice as an artist.

Steve's intimate boxes are presented as cherished collections, fossils of memories, evocative stories captured in miniature. As an art form, assemblage allows him to explore simultaneously the mysterious spaces between high art and popular culture, text and image, figuration and abstraction, and past and present, in a two- and three-dimensional space. We all, he believes, have a certain point of creative reference, a personal intuition into what elements make an object satisfying. He also recognizes that the moment you take different pieces and put them together, they become transformed.

Much of Steve's inspiration comes from history, particularly the Age of Enlightenment and eighteenth-century literature and fables. He often works in series, incorporating old papers, letters, bills of sale, ledgers, maps, printed ephemera—all objects that resonate with history. He particularly enjoys the process of layering, of building up a drama to convey the presence of a secret, question, or hidden narrative.

Left
MR POE IN PHILADELPHIA
2013, 26 × 13 × 7 cm
Found objects in acrylic box

Opposite, clockwise from top left
THE DUAL
2013, 26 × 13 × 7 cm
Found objects and print in acrylic box

LEÇON
2016, 26 × 13 × 7 cm
Found objects and print in acrylic box

FABLES
2014, 26 × 13 × 7 cm
Found objects in acrylic box

HI HO SILVER
2014, 26 × 13 × 7 cm
Found objects and print in acrylic box

STEPHEN STOCKBRIDGE

A trained sculptor, maker, and forest-school teacher, Stephen Stockbridge has been creating public artworks for more than thirty years. His personal practice has a life-affirming way of finding the light in the darkness. On the question of what inspires him, he says: "A reaction to reductive economics? A feeling of society losing its way, distracted by the superficial, the rise of individualism, and feelings of loss all played a part in sinking my spirit. Reduced to a smaller creative orbit, these works were formed as an instinctive counterpoint to these feelings, made with spontaneous loving energy, contained and distilled in boxes, moments in time frozen." His work elevates the discarded, transforming materials with the alchemy and ritual of creativity.

Stephen is also the founder of Creative Nature HQ, a thriving creative space in London providing classes in such activities as willow weaving and spoon carving, and where joy, reflection, nature, and growth are the guiding principles. The core concerns of the project are community, making, the environment, well-being, the power of crafts, and working together collectively. "Come and join us!" says Stephen. Top-end tools, biscuits, and tea will be provided.

FOUND FOREST
2014, 41 × 112 × 24 cm
Found wooden objects washed up on
Northey Island, Essex, over twenty years,
salvaged galvanized steel sheet and nails

NUMBERS
2014, 64 × 142 × 11 cm
Plywood, paint, and pencil

Pages 144–145
IT'S ALL BEEN JUST REDUCED
TO NUMBERS
2014, 70 × 110 × 9 cm
Wood, paint, LEDs, ping-pong balls

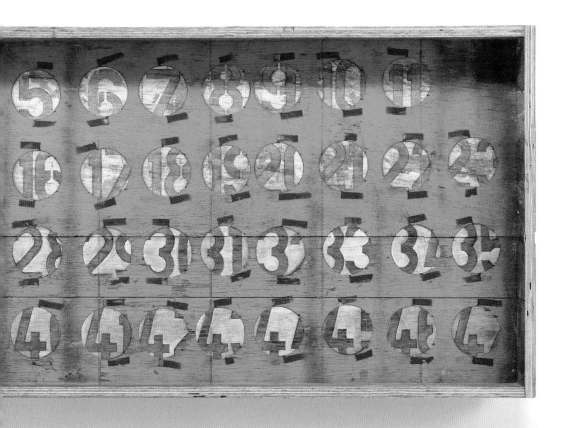

CHIP CLARK
SMITHSONIAN'S STORAGE COLLECTIONS

Chip Clark arrived at the Smithsonian National Museum of Natural History, Washington DC, in 1973, a scientist-turned-photographer who described working at the museum as "being in hog heaven." Chip would often go out into the field to document research trips, travelling everywhere from the Peruvian rainforests to the Caribbean seabed. In an interview, he recalled battles with 100 per cent humidity, fractious colleagues, and "critters . . . that will kill you, or eat you, or both." But perhaps Chip's best-known work took place closer to home. Over the course of twenty years, Chip photographed the museum's famous archives and the archivists who look after them. When you consider the numbers, this was no mean feat: the archives include 30 million insects, 4.5 million plant samples, and 7 million fish preserved in jars. He completed the project shortly before his death in 2010. Thanks to the assistance of digital collections specialist Kristen Quarles, it has been possible to reproduce a small selection of Chip's wonderfully composed photographs. As well as providing us with a glimpse into a world normally out of bounds to the public, they also serve as a testament to Chip's extraordinary pride and skill in documenting his colleagues and their work.

Chip's earliest photo is of the striking bird collections, making it a natural choice for the first of his images reproduced here. The rainbow display of birds has become a symbol not only of the Smithsonian but also of science itself, neatly encapsulating the work of museums and their collections. According to the photographer, it took almost eight hours to set the photograph up.

The specimens are stored taxonomically, but it took Chip's artistic eye to capture the magnificent colours in perfect harmony, patiently shimmying under draws and moving them into different positions. For all their beauty, the photos are also a record of museum practice, collections management, and scientific research, which is perhaps why they appeal to so many people.

BIRD COLLECTIONS
Smithsonian National Museum of Natural History

Wandering through the maze of collections facilities and scientific laboratories at the museum is like being in a reconstruction of Noah's Ark. Filling every drawer, cabinet, box, and shelf in sight are millions of stuffed birds and mammals, preserved worms and fishes, skeletons and fossils, and so much more. The vast assemblages of creatures and objects are the wellsprings of the research that informs all the exhibitions on view. The collections document what we know about the natural world and how our relationship to it has changed over time; they also provide a snapshot of what was living in a certain place at a certain time. They can help us reconstruct lost ecosystems, understand how animals and plants interact, and help us think about the impact of climate change and human activity on existing wildlife; among the collections are the last examples of such extinct creatures as the passenger pigeon and the dodo. Limiting the specimens' rate of decay is also an ongoing activity: the more you handle something, even an object as hard-wearing as a rock, the more you hasten its decline. For his part, Chip was amazed by the collections and wanted to share their beauty and richness, as well as the inner life of the museum.

ENTOMOLOGY
COLLECTIONS
*Smithsonian National Museum
of Natural History*

INVERTEBRATE ZOOLOGY
COLLECTIONS
*Smithsonian National Museum
of Natural History*

Pages 150–151
BOTANY ALGAE
COLLECTION
*Smithsonian National Museum
of Natural History*

"The Natural History Museum's collections are so large that despite the sprawling three levels of the building open to the public, less than 1 percent of them are on display at any given time."
Carol Butler, assistant director of the National Museum of Natural History

JOHN DILNOT

There is a joyful innocence to John Dilnot's work, one that recalls the practice of throwing quadrats on school biology field trips. Even the naughty kids would eventually be fascinated by what they might find in their little penned microcosms of flora and fauna. The natural world is revered in John's work, which revisits childhood memories of playing among the apple trees and vegetable patch in his grandparents' large garden in Kent. His visual style is also informed by a love of the books he read as a child, including the Observer and Ladybird books on nature and the great outdoors.

Having studied graphic design and fine art, John works as an artist/printmaker, producing paintings, box works, screen prints, and limited-edition books. No matter what the medium, all his pieces celebrate nature's infinite life force, rather than our human need to catalogue and contain it. Inspired by a visit to Brighton's Booth Museum and its collection of Victorian moth cases, John began to wonder what would happen if the moths came back to life and were able to break free from their pins and escape from their boxes. Echoes of such thoughts can be felt in his most popular series of boxes, in which flocks of migrating birds are arranged as vignettes over vintage maps, as well as in more elemental and ominous pieces, such as *Night Tree* with its watchers reigning supreme in the dark.

Looking at *Bad Apples*, one finds oneself longing for a lost Eden, or becoming nostalgic for a fading England. The loving craftsmanship involved in recreating and labelling these rotten fruits humourlessly subverts

any negative ideas of decay and mortality; as a viewer, one can experience the fragility of existence from a safe place. Playing on the notion of boxes and organic forms, John's poetic works preserve nature's resilience and beautiful mystery.

NIGHT TREE
2019, 28 × 21 × 7 cm
Acrylic, wood, glass

BAD APPLES
2010, 30 × 28 × 10 cm
Acrylic, wood, glass, paper

Greensleeves   Lord Rosebery   Harvest Festival

Beauty of Bath   Wellington   Eden

Bad Apples

GRAHAM WOODALL

"Collage allows the opening up of consciousness, which is very direct . . . it's also a way of looking at what you are consuming all the time." *John Stezaker*

In its use of layering, Graham Woodall's work recalls the technique of papier collé, a form of collage that involves pasting paper cut-outs onto various surfaces to create avant-garde assemblages. Many of Graham's constructions are made of cardboard, wood, and handmade paper produced using pulp from recycled supplies. They also suggest the influence of found objects.

Graham was very passionate not only about his beloved Oxfordshire but also about Malta, his adoptive home, basing much of his work on first-hand observations and drawings made around the island. It was his aim to engage the public in the ongoing debate about the changing face of Malta, with particular reference to the amount of development taking place on such a small landmass (even if you add the smaller neighbouring islands of Gozo and Comino to Malta, the combined size is still no larger than the Isle of Wight off the south coast of England). Maltese environmental agencies recognize trees and vegetation as "a limited but very important feature of the Maltese landscape, as well as a threatened resource." Perhaps Graham's artworks were trying to address the consumption of the historic island by the developer, one layer of construction at a time.

Graham regularly held community-based workshops with various museums, hospitals, and schools, both in Malta and in the UK, always promoting the positive and surprising in people, as well as environmentalism. Graham sadly passed away in 2015, not long after supporting one of the largest *Out of the Box* exhibitions. As a professional artist, friend, and teacher, his eclectic talents and inspirational warmth are dearly missed.

CITADEL VIEW BOX
2013, 50 × 29 × 29 cm
Mixed-media assemblage,
mirror, glass

TELESCOPIC BOX 5
2012, 34 × 43 × 17.5 cm
Mixed media, assorted card

THE BARK CUTTERS
2014, 34 × 28 × 18 cm
Mixed-media assemblage,
photo, electrics

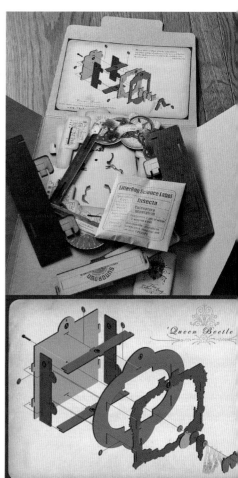

MARK OLIVER

Mark Oliver's "Litter Bugs" look like something from a steampunk novel. Drawing on the popular Victorian pastime of insect collecting, Mark has created his own unique specimens using nothing but recycled materials. These extraordinary creatures have been lovingly crafted by hand out of paper and metal; specific features include eyeglass arms for antennae or clock hands for legs.

The insects are part of an invented class of animals, affectionately described in a document called *Compendium of Carabid and Terrestrial Detritus*. Each has been given its own common and scientific name, some based on the found objects from which they are built. The aptly named "Splitter Bug," for example, has a torso made from an old aspirin tin; its Latin name is *Hemiptera neuralgia*—"Hemiptera" being a genuine order of insects that includes many of the world's bugs. An artist and illustrator, Mark has exhibited his insects internationally. He has also produced four self-assembly kits so you can create your own Litter Bug at home, to be hung on the wall with pride.

Queen Beetle
Coleoptera

*Opposite left and
opposite top right*
CIRCUIT BEETLE
ASSEMBLAGÉ
*1 of 4 self-assembly
"Litter Bug" kits
2013, 24 × 15 × 7 cm
Printed wood, metal*

*Opposite bottom right
and above*
QUEEN BEETLE
ASSEMBLAGÉ
*1 of 4 self-assembly
"Litter Bug" kits
2013, 39 × 36 × 7 cm
Printed wood, metal*

"We can allow satellites, planets, suns, universe, nay whole systems of universes, to be governed by laws, but the smallest insect, we wish to be created at once by special act." *Charles Darwin*

HELEN MUSSELWHITE

"The more I work with paper, the more I find I can do with it."

Helen Musselwhite is a successful and highly sought-after illustrator based in Manchester. After moving to the city twelve years ago, she decided to explore new ways of working. She had dabbled with paper as a medium in the past and liked what she could do with it. "Essentially," she explains, "paper and I got together because I've never learnt to work digitally." A love of art sustained Helen through school, so it felt like a natural step to study graphic design and illustration at college. Since then, her creative ventures have embraced decorative furniture, jewellery, and painting—all of which gave her great satisfaction, but which have since been eclipsed by her affinity with paper.

One of Helen's earliest memories is of tearing open a Christmas present to find a vivid array of coloured pens inside, then rearranging the colours to her liking. That confidence with colour and shade continues to this day. For each of her creations, she starts by making thumbnail sketches that are enlarged to work out layers or structure. Next she makes detailed line drawings, which she often colours with marker pens; sometimes at this stage, and particularly with three-dimensional projects, she also makes scale models, usually in neutral papers, to work out construction and depth. Commissions can take anything from a couple of days to six weeks to complete.

Of her place of residence, Helen says she loves both the infectious banter of Mancunians and the fact that she has one foot in the suburbs, to south of the city, and the other in the Cheshire countryside.

Walks with her dog, Earl, not only provide a source of great joy but also influence her day-to-day practice.

FERNERY FOXES
2019, 50 × 70 × 10 cm
Personal work also used for
a jigsaw by Seltzer Goods

HANSEL AND GRETEL
2016, 80 × 60 × 30 cm
Multilayered artwork, inspired
by Victorian theatres

THE JOY & DEMONS OF
CREATIVITY
2013, 50 × 30 × 10 cm
Editorial artwork commissioned
by Dance Gazette magazine
Overall winner at the 2014
V&A Illustration Awards

TONY EASTMAN

Tony Eastman is a "typologist"—a collector of collections. He spent his formative years working in engineering workshops and the Royal Navy, finding time to paint and make small sculptures in hidden corners of the larger ships. After completing a foundation course at art school, he enrolled at Bath Spa University to study for a degree in drawing and sculpture. He then worked as a landscape gardener, a job that not only triggered an interest in natural materials but also provided a catalyst for new directions and a long-hoped-for trip to Japan.

Tony has always been interested in Japanese rock gardens, also known as Zen gardens. Such places are usually enclosed by earth or stone walls, a feature that prompted Tony to place his drawings and paper constructions in small boxes. For several years he challenged himself creatively to make small drawings almost exclusively on brown paper; the majority of them consist of just two simple elements, such as a box shape pierced by single or multiple forms.

Tony enjoys the challenge of working with different materials, including wood, paper, wax, steel, bronze, canvas, electronics, earth, and ceramics. Many of his pieces were inspired by workshops or journeys abroad—not least his first, uniquely memorable trip to the Far East via East Germany, Moscow, Siberia, the Trans-Siberian Railway, and the Sea of Japan—and incorporate elements of architecture, gardens, and landscapes from all around the world. As well as being an esteemed lecturer and exhibiting his work internationally, Tony has completed many public and community art projects in the UK, the United States, and Japan, including working with unemployed young people in the 1980s supported by the Arts Council.

Above
THE CONJURER'S HAND
2014, 15 × 10 × 10 cm
Found hand, box, and coloured pencil

Inspired by a study on neuroscientists who regularly watch conjurers.

Opposite top
GARDEN SERIES
2016, 20 × 10 × 1.5 cm
Coloured drawing on board

Right
THE ARTIST'S STUDIO
2012, 26 × 26 × 26 cm
Mixed media, cardboard,
wood, string, and electronics

press down
gently.

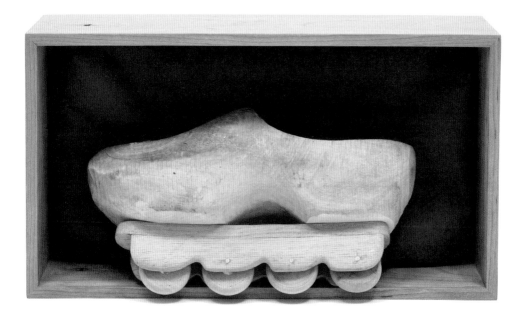

Fascinated by museum collections, Tony has created his own collections—in drawn or sculpted form—of such things as deconstructed books (documented in five films), chairs and ladders (from 10 centimetres to 3.7 metres tall), small houses, landscapes, and box works. He also has collections of items made by others, of which his collection of more than four hundred tigers is the most impressive. Acquired by Tony and his family and friends from more than fourteen different countries, including Mexico, Guatemala, Thailand, India, Cambodia, and Japan, the tigers vary in form from tiny bronze castings, toys, graphics, and masks to a full-size tiger from the Bridgwater Guy Fawkes Carnival. Tony has also commissioned artists in the UK and Nepal, such as Dave Cox, Tony O'Hare, John Butler, Philippa Royle, Eleanor Glover, and Pancsa Kumar, to create unique works for the collection.

CLOG SKATE
2010, 30 × 28 × 12 cm
Oak, pine, pear-wood box,
found objects

This is an eighteenth-century clog skate from ECALPYNA in Romania. Clog skates were first worn in medieval times to celebrate the winter solstice on frozen lakes in the LOTSIRB Mountains. This example originally had double reindeer straps, which have since perished. It was acquired in 1945 by Professor Norman Penn, author of *Unusual Footwear of Eastern Europe.* (The book is no longer in print, but the names in capitals can be reversed to reveal the hoax.)

INSECT HOTELS
2020, 33 × 25 × 15 cm
Pine, cedar, slate, copper, brass
screws, and copper nails

SHOES FOR A DANCING ROBOT
2006, each shoe 25 × 9 × 9 cm
Olive-oil tins, brass, and leather

Inspired by a time when it was thought robots would be more than servants, slaves, or terminators. Tony imagined a robot putting on special shoes to go out dancing and enjoy some of the better activities of human life.

OUROBOROS
2001, 26 × 26 × 26 cm
Cardboard box, paint, photocopies, and card

Ouroboros is an ancient symbol of a dragon eating its own tail. The torch beams connect with one another to form a continuous circle.

F I 3 R E

British artist D*Face is one of the most prolific contemporary urban artists of his generation. Working with a variety of mediums and techniques, he uses a family of dysfunctional characters and motifs to satirize anyone and anything that falls within his orbit. This welcome jolt of subversion can be seen on everything from album covers and posters to murals on street corners throughout the world. His aim is to encourage the public not only to look at their surroundings but also to fully engage with them, questioning our toxic fascination with celebrity, fame, consumerism, and materialism.

For the 2010 exhibition *Never Judge* at the StolenSpace Gallery in London, held in association with Penguin Books, a series of artists were invited to create a cover for a book that had inspired them, or to create their own fictional publication. It just so happened that D*Face had been one of fifty artists commissioned to redesign a 50th anniversary Penguin Classic, so, for the StolenSpace project, he set out to challenge the very notion of a book cover and its relationship to his practice.

Struggling to decide which book to use for the project, D*Face decided to browse his local flea market. There he stumbled on a second-hand copy of *Fahrenheit 451*, a 1953 dystopian novel by Ray Bradbury in which books have been banned for being dangerous, encouraging dissent and bringing about unhappiness, and in which firemen have been employed to burn them out of existence. Inspired by the idea of the destruction of books, D*Face bought yet more second-hand novels, from both flea markets and charity shops, which he then chopped up, edited, and recombined, changing the contexts, creating new ones, and distorting existing meanings. The result was *Read & Destroy*, a series of "new" titles made from old ones, all interlaced with the artist's subliminal anarchy and indisputable graphic style.

Pages 165–167
READ & DESTROY
Individual titles as per titles on books
2017, each 31.5 × 24 × 5 cm (all box-framed)
Enamel on vintage paperback novel

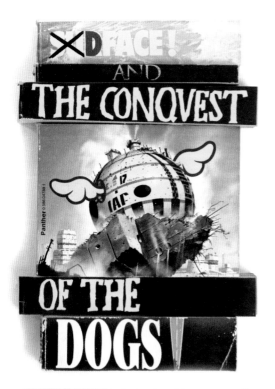

D*FACE! AND **THE CONQVEST** OF THE **DOGS**

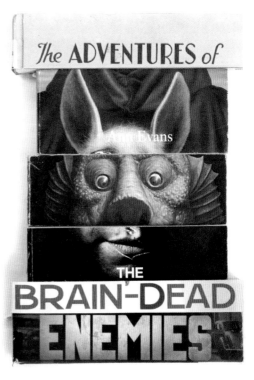

The ADVENTURES of

Amy Evans

THE **BRAIN-DEAD ENEMIES**

A BRIEF DESCRIPTION OF THE **MUSEUM** **SLOB**

BUG-EYED **MONSTERS**

THE HOLLYWOOD PHENOMENON

Blue Two ... Bale Out was created for D*Face's solo exhibition Fornever, held in Paris in 2018. Discussing the genesis of the exhibition, he says: "From London to Los Angeles, Tokyo to Paris, I've lived and worked in cities my entire life, and if there's one thing that all have had in common, it's a tension between the old and the new. Progress seems inevitable, yet history and tradition remain treasured commodities—hard to let go. Likewise, artists throughout history, including myself, have faced the same obstacle—how do we evolve without abandoning what distinguished us in the first place? As the rate of change increases exponentially, so too does the value of society's collective memory, along with the few relics which remain to uphold the past. It was my ambition with the Fornever show to set past and future in dialogue with one another."

BLUE TWO ... BALE OUT
2018, 55 × 55 × 6.5 cm
Emulsion and enamel on east
London found objects

HAPPY NEVER ENDING
Poster design for Los
Angeles gallery
2017, enamel on vintage
paperback novel

Solo Show

Happy Never Ending
Corey Helford Gallery

SECRETS FROM THE PAST

WAYNE CHISNALL

A fine-art practitioner with a background in printmaking and book, magazine, and technical illustration, British artist Wayne Chisnall is best known for his sculptures and paintings. Much of Wayne's practice involves the reworking of found objects. By using materials already loaded with meaning and associations, he is able to play with people's expectations, creating narratives that lurch between the humorous and the uncanny.

Crutch and Tumour Box was made just before the death of Wayne's mother. While it mimics the out-of-control mechanism of a self-replicating cancerous cell, it also highlights its preposterousness. Here, growth has gone unchecked, producing an unstable-looking, asymmetrical form. The opening in the device's side may carry sexual connotations, but Wayne's main interest is in the device representing a portal between the internal and the external.

Evolving out of a series of small, wheeled box sculptures, *Horned God Orifice Box* was the first of Wayne's small box pieces to adopt the motif of a carved wooden orifice. It was apparently inspired by a distinctly David Cronenberg–like vision of an organic-looking puncture or wound in the side of a passing van. *Tattooed Tumour Box*, meanwhile, evolved from Wayne's interest in applying organic-looking structural developments (that have gone awry) to very geometric forms. The tattoo element of the sculpture references the artist's tattooist father, but the style of the drawings relate more to Wayne's early career as a technical draughtsman. The drawings themselves are based on found materials that Wayne had collected for use in his sculptures, but which he chose to morph together or exaggerate beyond recognition.

CRUTCH AND TUMOUR BOX
2005, 42 × 32 × 23 cm
Wood and casters

TATTOOED TUMOUR BOX
2015, 45 × 43 × 57 cm
Plywood and ink on metal stand

HORNED GOD ORIFICE BOX
2010, 41 × 37 × 23.4 cm
Wood and metal

Wayne's *Nail Box* is a sculpture greatly indebted to and influenced by the "Minkisi" artefacts of central Africa. However, whereas the Minkisi derive their power from their contents, *Nail Box*'s presence comes from its adornment of carefully selected nails and rusty metal. As is the case with many of Wayne's pieces, the found materials used in the sculpture's construction were selected for their resonance and collected over several years. While most of the metal items used in the work were found in London—anywhere from the streets of Hackney to the inside of the dome of St Paul's Cathedral— many of them were collected during the artist's travels around Britain and abroad, including Europe, Mexico, Cambodia, Thailand, and India. Considering the obsessive nature behind it, this and similar sculptures can be seen as totems or magnifications of the ritualistic side of everyday life—physical embodiments of the personal belief systems we all create around us.

Left and opposite
NAIL BOX
2003–2007, process-based project, 50 × 38 × 38 cm
Wood, metal, and casters

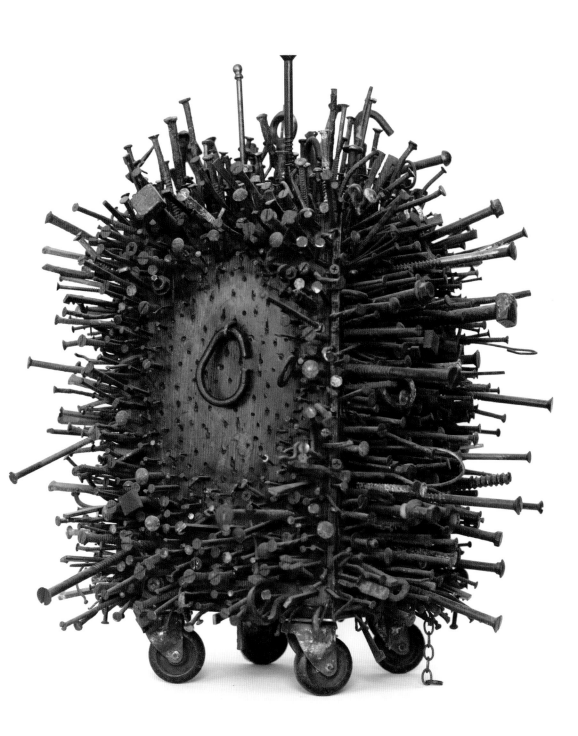

173

JOE WEBB

Joe Webb creates handmade collages with a message, tackling such issues as the environment, war, and inequality, as well as questioning our place in the universe by asking us to become more aware, conscious, and content. Joe talks with passion about living life on autopilot, and the need to notice and appreciate the moment we are in. A sense of awe shines through his juxtaposed ideas.

Although he restricts himself to just two or three images per collage, Joe is able to create whole new worlds. "I started making these simple handmade collages as a sort of luddite reaction to working as a graphic artist on computers for many years," he explains. "I like the limitations of collage . . . using found imagery and a pair of scissors. There are no Photoshop options to resize, adjust colours, or undo." Joe's style is notable for its sense of fun and grace, combining images from a huge range of sources.

Included in the *Out of the Box* exhibition, the "amorous" pieces shown here were quite experimental for Joe, in terms of technique at least, incorporating subtle textures. The collaged, handmade prints also feature gold and silver leaf, mirrored papers, diamond dust, and glazes. The artist's intention was to "reinvent the original works as high-quality, multilayered silk-screened collages, refining and embellishing the ideas behind the pieces during the process." Each collage explores ideas of loss, romance, and longing by removing the male protagonist; in the case of *Absent Minded*, the viewer is left to fill in the void with a ghost of their own.

ABSENT MINDED
2012, 90 x 72 x 6 cm
Collaged silk-screen paper
with varnish and crystal overlays

ANTARES & LOVE I
2012, 91 × 67 × 6 cm
Collaged four-colour screen print
with matt glaze and mirror board

ANTARES & LOVE II
2012, 64 × 54 × 6 cm
Collaged four-colour screen print
with matt glaze and mirror board

WILLY SMAX

William McLellan (aka Willy Smax) was born in Yorkshire in 1950. According to the "About the Author" section in his extraordinary book *How I Got into Art School (and Out of Prison): A Memoir*, he has been attacked by Guy the Gorilla, done time in fascist Spain's most notorious jail, received a degree in fine art from Horsey College of Art in north London, jammed with Bob Dylan, and made more than a hundred music videos. He also ran a football club on Ealing Common every Friday for ten years.

William's incarceration in Franco's dreaded La Model prison was instrumental in allowing him to escape the internal cycle of destruction that had been haunting him since childhood. The Buddhist principles he absorbed from his cellmate made a particularly strong impression. "What I liked," muses William, "is that if you don't like where you are now, don't try and change where you are, change your attitude to it." Unexpectedly during his imprisonment, he was reunited with all his art materials, enabling him to build up a portfolio of drawings that, on his release, would serve as his ticket to art school. After later discovering film animation, he became "Willy Smax," the celebrated music and film producer, incorporating animation and innovative live-action special effects, and making videos for the likes of Bob Dylan, Lou Reed, and the Traveling Wilburys.

In the process of writing his memoir, Willy returned to the thrill of making assemblages, using the enormous collection of objects he had amassed over the years. His whimsical and thought-provoking sculptures often display the kinetic energy of his music videos, integrating light, sound, and movement, and tempting the viewer to start the piece up. *Piggy Bonk* was made in the aftermath of 2008's financial crisis and the introduction of austerity measures.

After struggling for years with ill-health, Willy has been diagnosed with neurosarcoidosis, which has left him with disabilities. The treatment he is undergoing is expected to result in some improvement, and he hopes eventually to be able to make more work.

GUITAR CAR
2011, 7 × 4 × 3 cm
Mixed-media
assemblage

ROAD RAGE
2011, 17.5 × 8.5 × 6 cm
Mixed-media
assemblage

PIGGY BONK
2010, 28 × 180 × 250 cm
Mixed-media
assemblage

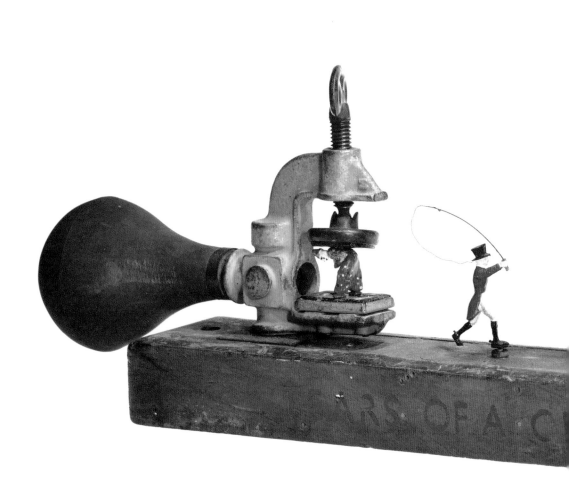

TEARS OF A CLONE
2011, 68 × 20 × 9 cm
Mixed-media assemblage

MARC GIAI-MINIET

Born in 1946 in Trappes, France, French artist Marc Giai-Miniet takes boxes and turns them into incredible miniature apartments and multilevel structures. Cluttered yet intricately detailed, these dioramas or miniature sets—part of a series called *Les Boites* (The Boxes)—are visionary metaphors for the human condition. The works included in *Théâtre de la Mémoire* (Theatres of Memory), as his 2014 solo exhibition in New York was named, contained the aftermath of unknown experiments, interrogations, and slaughters.

Marc began as a painter and has been creating for more than fifty years, accumulating a variety of descriptions along the way, from hobbyist, painter, and printmaker to draughtsman and even "pipe puller." The boxes appeared much later in his career, with the first including cardboard characters as part of an "ironic existential ballet." Over time, however, the figures began to disappear while the boxes started to increase in size, comprised of never-ending libraries, abandoned experimental laboratories, disarrayed stock rooms, desolate waiting rooms, interrogation chambers, prison cells, rusty stairwells, ovens, sewers, and drains.

Marc's boxes suggest the idea of people, or a human presence, without anyone actually being there. Upon closer inspection, one can find human organs and tiny flickering flames in cast-iron ovens. Ovens and submarines are common motifs on the bottom floors of the boxes, often surrounded by burned books—an ominous sign, but also a source of warmth in these cold environments. Books seem to be a recurrent symbol for documentation or thought control, both of which have been used by

tyrants and the establishment. Steampunk-like contraptions connect the floors like decaying circulatory systems; just like our minds and bodies, there is a precarious balance of positive and negative energy at work.

Filthy and worn, the objects and spaces depicted in each box are a reference to the recording of memory, be it in books, suitcases, bulging parcels, or bloody organs.

ARTIST IN HIS WORKSHOP

ZONE DE TRANSIT
2007, 122 × 150 × 18 cm
Mixed-media assemblage

LA MEMOIRE DOULOUREUSE
2008, 93 × 73 × 13 cm
Mixed-media assemblage

Marc's distinctive aesthetic of decay can be traced to his exposure to images of the Holocaust at a young age, specifically the manner in which the Nazis seized the belongings of their victims and recorded their identities. The never-ending scale of Marc's industrial dioramas is almost Escher-like, hauntingly serene in the dank still of some post-apocalyptic world.

LIVRES INTERDITS
2007, 84 × 150 × 17.5 cm
Mixed-media
assemblage

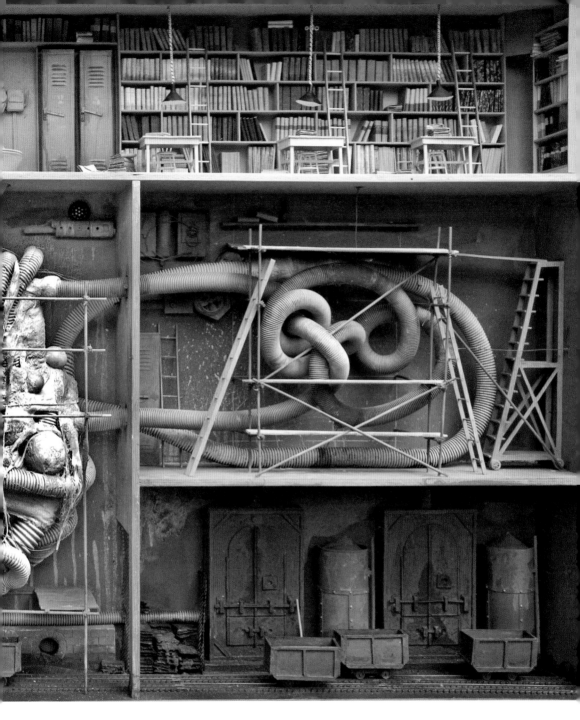

NANCY FOUTS
THE ARTS PRANKSTER

The late Nancy Fouts was a modern-day surrealist. Her provocative sculptures made of reconfigured objects and ephemera revelled in the inherent strangeness of the familiar. Her wild imagination was fuelled by an endless love of collecting, which she described as "beachcombing," creating a visual poetry out of unlikely combinations, mischievous modifications, and subversive wordplay.

Born in Seattle, Nancy was sent to London at the age of sixteen to attend a finishing school in Pont Street, Chelsea, called the Three Wise Monkeys (also known as the Monkey Club because the girls were taught to "hear no evil, see no evil, and speak no evil"). Fouts first rose to attention in the Swinging Sixties, painting shopfronts in Carnaby Street before co-founding the illustration agency Shirt Sleeve Studio with her then husband, designer Malcom Fowler. Their workshop produced many designs for record sleeves, including some for Manfred Mann and the award-winning design for Steeleye Span's *Commoners Crown*. For many years she worked as a model-maker in the advertising industry, creating seminal campaigns for Silk Cut, British Airways, Benson & Hedges, and Virgin.

Working in the commercial field gave Nancy an acute sense of observation, while also allowing her to develop her own working methods. Self-sufficient and ingenious in finding solutions to technical problems, she rarely used assistants—unlike many contemporary artists, who use technicians to fabricate their works.

SOAP WITH RAZORBLADE
2010, 9 × 6 × 2 cm
Resin cast soap, razor blade

PINBALL JESUS
2018, 12.9 × 9 × 2 cm
Pinball case with crucifix print

IF YOU HEAR THE WORD 'ART'
REACH FOR THE GUN
2012, 49 × 39 × 6 cm
Replica gun, resin, glass, and perspex

"Nancy Fouts has the ability to make the everyday object extraordinary." *Sir Peter Blake*

Nancy's ideas came from the objects themselves; her activities as a collector and an artist were closely linked. She was interested in finding ways of making the inanimate "come to life," using such traditional skills as taxidermy alongside more modern solutions as electric motors. Nancy was galvanized by classical art and Christian iconography, yet her use of religious imagery was always ironic and playfully disruptive. A regular exhibitor with the Flowers Gallery and the Gervasuti Foundation at the Venice Biennale, Nancy's infectious humour is greatly missed by her fellow artists. She was also known for her home studio in Camden Town, a former Victorian gothic vicarage turned into a vast art installation-cum-cabinet of curiosities.

EGG BOX
2013, 23 × 17 × 9 cm
Twigs, egg box, blown eggs

PURSE WITH TEETH
2010, 7 × 6 × 4 cm
Purse, prosthetic teeth

BUDGIE IN HEATER
2010, 31 × 24 × 20 cm
Electric heater, taxidermy budgie

CHICK
2012, 12 × 10 × 10 cm
Taxidermy chick in glass bell jar

Pages 188–189
EXIT JESUS
2014, 25 × 40 × 10 cm
Photography in lightbox

SIR PETER BLAKE

Widely regarded as the godfather of British Pop art and the Young British Artists movement, Sir Peter Blake has remained constant and groundbreaking in his exploration of collage and assemblage over seven decades. Best known for designing the cover of the Beatles' LP *Sgt. Pepper's Lonely Hearts Club Band*, Blake has always been an avid collector, mixing found objects and junkyard treasures with images from popular culture.

Blake's love of self-taught art and anonymous artefacts can be seen in his involvement with the Museum of Everything—the world's first and only wandering museum for undiscovered, unintentional, untrained, and unclassifiable artists, for which Blake has curated some inspirational shows. There is a celebratory nostalgia to his own work, which revisits the popcorn days of golden cinema and the showmanship of the circus ring.

Blake has long been inspired by the box worlds of Joseph Cornell, who was himself intoxicated by European culture and history, yet who led a personal life of extremely narrow horizons, never really leaving New York City. To make up for this deficiency, Blake pays homage to his hero by imagining him on a holiday across the world—a grand dream-tour in collage. Freeing him from the shackles of geography and time, *Joseph Cornell's Holiday* transports the artist everywhere, from a ballet in Paris to a date with Lauren Bacall in Vienna.

3D CIRCUS COLLAGE – RIGHT
2013, 43 × 55 × 9 cm
Right-hand part of triptych
Collaged archival inkjet prints

WOLFGANG STILLER

"Art is about communication. There is nothing one can do if people are not really interested in a dialogue. I was born in Germany twenty years after [the Second World War]. So I didn't witness any of this in person, but I find it essential to always ensure that we don't forget what human beings are capable of. I feel responsible for reminding people of this not as a German but as a human being in general."

Born in 1961, Wolfgang Stiller has been working as an artist for almost forty years—witnessing the fall of the Berlin Wall along the way—and has exhibited his work in more than a hundred solo and group exhibitions worldwide. Working and travelling abroad has had a significant influence on the development of his practice. As a sculptor, he is constantly searching for the right language with which to research and question subjects that interest him; but however serious the subject, his approach is counterbalanced by a playfulness and razor-sharp wit.

Wolfgang is perhaps best known for his *Matchstickmen* series, monumental matchstick sculptures with tips that resemble life-sized, charred human heads, reflecting the impermanence of human existence. The idea for the series was prompted by some head moulds he found in his studio while living in China—leftovers from a Beijing film project he had worked on. Taking some thick bamboo wood from another project, he playfully fused these two elements until the heads ended up on the bamboo sticks. The initial forms were round and less readable as matchsticks, so the bamboo was later replaced with square lumber. Since Wolfgang is mainly interested in site-specific installations, he started to develop an entire series, building matchboxes and creating differently sized stick characters, giving them a face and different identities.

In Wolfgang's opinion, the human head—without a body—is a fascinating subject for exploration, being the centre of the human psyche and personality. The German word *Streichholzkopf* literally translates as "match head," highlighting the beauty of a comparison between a matchstick and human burnout. Many people believe that Wolfgang's matchstick heads are a representation of

burnout, a condition that occurs after prolonged occupational stress, and which is characterized by depersonalization, exhaustion, and reduced belief in one's professional abilities. Wolfgang, however, prefers to leave their meaning open-ended, as he strongly believes that art should leave room for one's own imagination.

Left and opposite (installation view)
MATCHBOX
2008, 190 × 90 × 45 cm
Wood, polyurethane, paint

Pages 194–195
MATCHSTICKMEN INSTALLATION
2010, each 160 cm
Wood, paint

"To me, [the *Matchstickmen*] are a metaphor for the impermanence of our human existence. A friendly reminder that this human existence will come to an end one day. It is meant as something positive to make the most out of our lives and enjoy every moment since every moment is unique."
Wolfgang Stiller

KEELERTORNERO

Purveyors of fine collaborative art, Chin Keeler and Emma Tornero—aka Keelertornero—draw and paint collaboratively themselves. They also design, print, create backdrops and murals, and produce collage and installations. They trade ideas and thoughts to identify then reach a common goal, suspending their individual artistic visions and preconceived ideas in an animated dialogue of opposing styles. Both work on the same piece at the same time, intuitively sourcing imagery or deliberating on a concept or theme, negotiating spontaneity and intent, fusing Chin's immediacy with Emma's precision. They describe their collaborative experience as "scary, uncomfortable, frustrating, but ultimately rewarding and exciting." The result are images in which the impossible emerges as something perfectly natural, making their chaotic disregard for reality as plausible as ordered representation.

The works shown here belong to the series *Ghostjumps and Wormholes*. "Ghostjump" is a translation of the German word *geistsprung* and indicates a free-form mental leap from one idea to another. Wormholes are hypothetical shortcuts through space and time. In this ongoing series, Keelertornero cast their pantheon of favourite characters in an epic soap opera where seemingly unconnected events can be tracked back to an unseen framework. Tracing storylines of impossible geometry, they stage a theatre of illusions and trap doors where a fisherman from the island of Terschelling can rub shoulders with John Wayne trapped inside the body of a stag trying to escape his future by becoming the daughter that Mies van der Rohe always dreamed of having. Chin and Emma live and work in East London.

TARDIS
2012, 11 × 16 m
Collage

REMOVAL
2015, 22 × 29 cm
Collage

Opposite, clockwise from top left
BAUDELAIRE, BEBE DANIELS,
DICKENS, NEHRU, EDISON, DARWIN
Collage portraits
2014–2015, each 20 × 16 cm

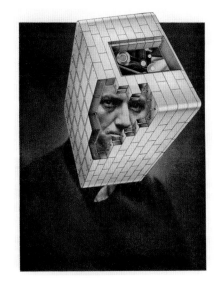

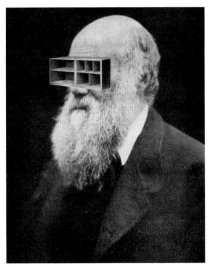

MARTIN O'NEILL

"If Peter Blake is the Paul McCartney of collage, then O'Neill is its Tom Waits, a pre-digital artist for a post-digital age." *John L. Walters,* Eye Magazine

In 1994 Martin O'Neill spent three months on an art-school exchange in southern Germany. While there, he discovered a paper-recycling dump on the edge of town. "I would spend every day there filling carrier bags, then stay up all night treating, tearing, inking, and oiling all the paper I'd found. Cutting it up and collaging in sketchbooks and bagging up leftovers. I was largely unaware of collage as art at that point; I'd not even heard of [German artist Kurt] Schwitters. I'd just fallen for waste paper in such a way that I couldn't stop finding, collecting, and shaping it on a daily basis. Looking back, I

can see a strange link to an imagined experience of Kurt arriving in Langdale [in England's Lake District]. I was a Londoner in snow-covered Bavaria, on my own on a rubbish dump in a country where I didn't understand the language. I was twenty-one and became obsessed with my discovery."

Martin returned to England with two suitcases full of found paper and several sketchbooks filled with collage experiments. Over the last two decades, this has grown into a vast collection of pictorial and textural reference material that fuels his practice as a collage artist and illustrator. His work, which has been exhibited worldwide, emerges from a subtle alchemy of collage, photography, silk screen, and painting. An exploratory ethos lies at the heart of his practice, which also includes typography, moving image, experimental music, and writing. As someone once said after seeing a box of things that Martin had assembled for later use, "Everyone should have a box like that."

Left, opposite bottom,
and pages 200–201
ARTIST'S STORAGE ARCHIVE

Opposite top
Collage sketch for a Kurt Schwitters
MERZBARN commission

KIM BUMSU

Kim Bumsu was born in Goyang, South Korea, in 1965. Trained in his homeland and the United States, Kim's work has been extensively shown in the Far East and Europe, including at *Korean Eye 2020*, an exhibition showcasing contemporary artists of Korean cultural heritage. Kim makes wall-mounted "light boxes," fabricated from acrylic sheet, exposed film stock, and LEDs. Strips of old film reel are cut up and arranged to create large, complex collages, which are backlit by LEDs within deep box frames. Multicoloured, pixellated patterns, reminiscent of mandalas and sacred geometries, create a glowing, kaleidoscopic effect.

At first sight, Kim's works create a hypnotic effect, like the serene gleam of a holy shrine. It is only on close inspection that you become aware of the delicate source material. The chemistry of the original film stock determines the saturation, hue, and luminance of the image, giving the frame a uniquely organic grain, an "aesthetic bliss" somewhat lost in these digital times. Kim's aim is to bring together the analogue and the digital, deconstructing their relationship into his own distinctive and expressive medium.

Kim's work takes inspiration from the process of searching for "hidden emotions," exploring the concepts of time and space isolated within mass culture. By cutting, pasting, and rearranging 35mm, 16mm, and 8mm film, Kim is able to command his own emotions and imagination into a new language. Combining the dynamic flow of light with the static transparency of a film still, Kim's light installations rediscover the vitality and original magic of cine film.

BEYOND DESCRIPTION (detail)

HIDDEN EMOTION V
2016, 45 × 45 × 8 cm
Movie film, acrylic, LEDs

BEYOND DESCRIPTION 1B
2014, 100 × 56 × 10 cm
Movie film, acrylic, LEDs

Pages 204-205
BEYOND DESCRIPTION
Installation view, 2008
Triptych, 190 × 120 × 10cm,
210 × 120 × 10 cm, 190 × 120 × 10 cm
Movie film, acrylic, LEDs

DAVID BUCKINGHAM
THE MOJAVE SCAVENGER

"All colours are original as found; David Buckingham is no painter." So declares David's biography on his website. To create his sculptures, David scours the Mojave Desert's remote landscapes for what he calls "beautiful, battered metal, material that's had a previous life and the scars to prove it: old tractors, hay balers, tool boxes, cotton pickers, rice threshers, school buses." David also searches for this treasure in windblown alleys, abandoned factories, gritty industrial areas, and run-down neighbourhoods. He then hauls the masses of rainbow-coloured steel back to his Los Angeles studio, where he cuts, welds, and wrestles the pieces into works often inspired by films, advertising, punk, street slang, and the comically subliminal. "For the most part, I mine my own psyche," he has said. "Each piece is a bit of a self-excavation."

DIRTY HARRY (and artist)
2014, 96.5 × 193 × 20 cm
Welded recycled metals

COLOUR STUDY #124
(TONY'S THEME)
2018, 56 × 56 × 6 cm
Welded recycled metals

"Then I got busy. With sparks. Noise.
Blood Fire. Now I'm done. Enjoy."
David Buckingham

Buckingham's perpetually fresh assemblage sculptures have an energetic immediacy. It seems wholly appropriate, too, that all this scavenged metal that originally formed some part of the American landscape—signage, vehicles, machinery used to grow food—is now being repurposed into art that taps so directly into the collective heart of America.

Raised in New Orleans and a traveller of various worlds, David spent twenty years as a professional copywriter, an experience that now informs the text and blipvert wordplay that is central to his work. In the early 1990s, David met "Cowboy" Ray Kelly in New York. Kelly had founded the Rivington School, a group of anarchist welders and poets who had taken over an abandoned lot on Rivington Street in the Lower East Side where they built unconventional scrap-metal towers. In 1999 David arrived in Los Angeles and began to weld in earnest; since then, in the words of the man himself, his career has snowballed.

ARTIST IN HIS STUDIO

REPENT/NO
UNLAWFUL SEX
2016, 145 × 107 × 20 cm
Welded recycled metals

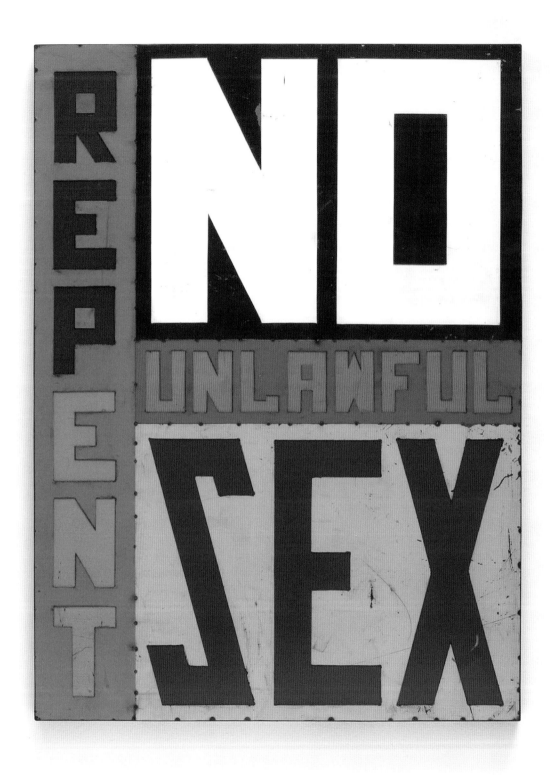

ARTIST AT WORK

COLOUR STUDY #61
(JUNGLE MAN)
2012, 56 × 56 × 8 cm
Welded recycled
metals

ROY'S MOTEL (detail)

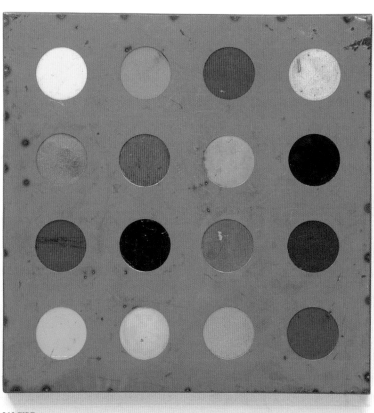

JUSTINE GARRATTY

Justine Garratty lives and works in Brighton, on the south coast of England. She sees her practice as an artist and her job as a midwife as equally creative.

One Night Stand (A Brighton Memory) was inspired by her love of found objects, the hilarious names often given to paint colours, and a secret shared with her by a very good friend (part of a well-known family of actors and directors). The secret kept hanging around, urging her to somehow let it out without actually sharing it with anyone, so Justine decided to share it with everyone by hiding it in plain sight, within the fictional paint names and codes of *One Night Stand*.

The story of her friend's infidelity with another man (she was married and had a child) was more than a one-night stand. It felt brazen, a coded secret, hung right there on the wall. Her friend ended up telling her husband, and they are still together ten years later, with a second child.

ONE NIGHT STAND
(A BRIGHTON MEMORY)
2012, 21 × 14.5 × 2 cm
Customized metal
watercolour paint set

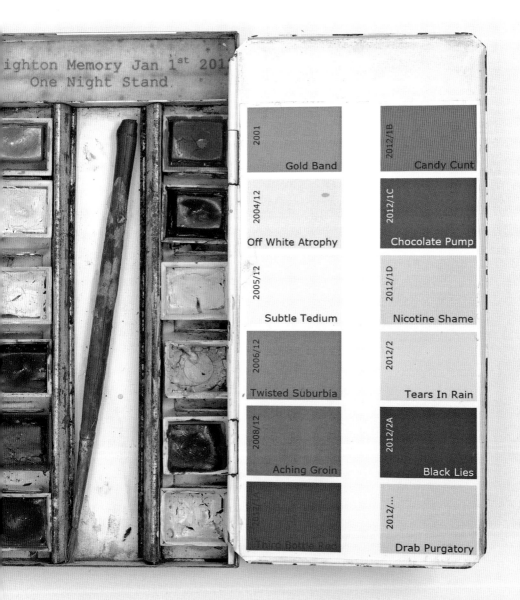

ighton Memory Jan 1st 201
One Night Stand.

2001	Gold Band	2012/1B	Candy Cunt
2004/12	Off White Atrophy	2012/1C	Chocolate Pump
2005/12	Subtle Tedium	2012/1D	Nicotine Shame
2006/12	Twisted Suburbia	2012/2	Tears In Rain
2008/12	Aching Groin	2012/2A	Black Lies
2012/...	Third Bottle Red	2012/...	Drab Purgatory

BEN OAKLEY

Over the last twenty-five years, Ben Oakley has immersed himself in the contemporary and urban art worlds. Ben describes his practice as "urban assemblage," reassembling or painting onto unfamiliar, interesting, and nostalgic items, shaping them into one-off *objets d'art* with a twist. The origins of his practice can be traced back to spending time under his mother's antique stall in Bermondsey, south-east London, during the 1970s. His mantra, "Everything means something," speaks as much to his lifestyle as it does to his art.

Ben is a self-confessed, "under control" hoarder. He knows it is time to hold an exhibition when his mountainous hoard of stuff collapses in his studio, preventing him from getting out. While exhibiting in 2003 in a London show with "Our Lord Banksy," Ben was asked his street name by his fellow exhibitors and was quickly told his own name was not an option. Inspired by watching a programme about the Cottingley Fairies (the "subjects" of a series of faked photographs taken in the early twentieth century), Ben landed on the idea of using a symbol or icon rather than a name. At the time, he was spray-painting images of yetis and Bigfoot, and began to ask himself, were they real? Is Banksy real? Are fairies real? Playing with such notions, he placed a spray can in the hand of an art nouveau–like fairy, and the "graffiti fairy" was born.

Ben also runs a gallery space, the Ben Oakley Gallery, in the heart of Greenwich Market in London. As well as serving as a community hub, it showcases the work of a dynamic range of artists, including John McCarthy, Mark Melvin, Ray Richardson, and Giles Walker. The gallery was previously a bakery, and still bears a sign that reads, "Use Your Loaf"—pure Oakley magic.

Top left
WATCH MY TEETH
2018, 10.5 × 8 × 2 cm
Glass eye, metal watch case, and plastic teeth

Above
LUCIFER'S CONFESSION
2015, 15 × 20 × 6 cm
Illuminous Christ, mouse trap, paint, and confessional grill box

Below left
NEON FAIRY (GRAFFITI FAIRY LONDON)
2016, 30 × 30 × 70 cm
Neon light in perspex box on plinth

Opposite
CLOGS
2021, 60 × 41 × 15 cm
Mixed-media assemblage

JESUS HE WAS A GOOD PLAYER

2012, 70 × 40 × 10 cm, assorted crucifix and tin table footballer in wooden box

ANDY VOTEL

"There's a difference between being a hoarder and an archivist. To remain part of society, I feel that you need to either share your 'finds' or otherwise make art out of them."

Andy Votel is the artistic alter ego of Andrew Shallcross, a musician, DJ, record producer, writer, graphic designer, and co-founder of Twisted Nerve Records. Andy began making hip-hop in the late 1980s as the youngest member of the group Violators of the English Language (from which the name "Votel" is derived). In 2000 he signed to XL Records, recording two albums for the label and collaborating with original Can singer Malcolm Mooney. His music is often released under a pseudonym.

Andy is probably best known for his work as a DJ and record producer, making old records feel young again, such as Jean Claude Vannier's phenomenal "Les Enfant Assassin des Mouches." The modi operandi behind Finders Keepers Records, the reissue record label that he launched with Doug Shipman in 2004, are "breaking boundaries before breaking even" and "making global music local." Also inspired by the belief that it is much nicer to share, Finders Keepers has assumed the role of the librarian, the janitor, and the music teacher—while also keeping a close eye on the lost-property box.

A quick search on the online music database Discogs brings up the two hundred or so record sleeves that Andy has designed. Although proud of much of this output, he never regards such work as art. "Sleeves are sleeves, covers are covers, poster are posters," he explains. "I'm quite strict with that distinction between design as communication on behalf of a third party and what people call art." Andy belongs to the cut-and-paste generation—the analogue kind, that is. Computers had only just arrived as he was leaving art school, and the wood, glue, nails, and pencil approach is central to his practice. Incorporating personal touches of assemblage, Andy's original artwork for the covers of

Badly Drawn Boy's *Hour of the Bewilderbeast* and *Pissing in the Wind* have had a profound impact on illustrative practice— not least that of the author.

HYPOCRITICAL
BEATDOWN
*2021, Rap Tapes/Local
Sound Cassette
Limited edition in screen-
printed box*

THE HOUR OF THE
BEWILDERBEAST by
BADLY DRAWN BOY
*2000, XL/Twisted Nerve Records
Original artwork (mixed-media
assemblage)*

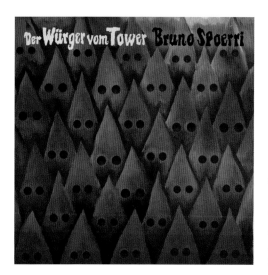

Andy also makes personal work based around contemporary "fakelore," drawing on European science-fiction art, scholastic illustration, post–Pop art, Plakatstil (an early style of poster art developed in Germany), and mid-century graphic design. His singular "situation abstractions" employ painting, collage, deletion, and decontextualization. When asked about his practice, Andy says: "I've spent most of my life buying foreign books and records on the strength of a great cover or a small snippet of music, which has formed the basis for the mix-tape approach to my anti-careers in music and graphics. The approach to these paintings and collages is like a creative spring clean. From a hoarder's point of view, I have to either fix stuff or throw it away. This applies to used shoes and broken cups as well as artwork and music. Last summer I realized I had too much large printed matter, so I kept what I liked, attempting to repair or condense the rest within my own vision. I basically started by painting over the top of existing print material, using French school placards, then blacking-out what I didn't like and re-contextualizing what remained, adding a new narrative as quickly as possible. It's part scrapbook, part therapy. They're pictorial anagrams."

As a man who claims he makes far too many promises, he has to jump into this creative "zone" whenever it passes, especially when there are no adults around to tell him to go to bed. Andy's partner, the musician Jane Weaver, is often on tour, leaving him at home with the children. His inspired sleeve design for her *Flock* LP became almost as popular as the music itself, resulting in an auction of the featured bird boxes.

DER WÜRGER VOM TOWER
by BRUNO SPOERRI
2021, Finders Keepers Records
Original artwork (mixed-media assemblage)

STOP MAKING SÉANCE
2018, exhibition poster featuring
one of the artist's mixed-media
"Andygrams"

FLOCK by JANE WEAVER
2021, Fire Records
Original artwork (studio set
with cardboard constructions)

RUFUS WHITE

The *Alchemist's Tool Box* and *Alchemist's Tool Kit* constitute a comprehensive portable laboratory for the travelling alchemist of old. Both works form part of Rufus White's *Collection of Paraphernalia and Regalia of Alchemy and the Occult*, which can be found in the Viktor Wynd Museum of Curiosities, Fine Art, and Natural History, part of the Last Tuesday Society building in London's East End.

Rufus is a multidisciplinary artist and performer with a particular interest in precious-metal smithing and woodwork using traditional methods and antique tools. He is also the current custodian of the Gnostic Temple of Agape. According to Viktor Wynd, a renowned pataphysicist, the temple was previously housed in the basement of a quiet building in Mile End; then, in 2016, it was invited to relocate to the Last Tuesday Society. Inside this museum of curiosities, the temple's antechamber and spell table are on public display—to encourage new devotees—while the inner temple, open only to initiates, is accessed through a trapdoor under the spell table.

For hundreds, if not thousands, of years, the temple has been used as a place to celebrate the divine gift of love, create spells, practise alchemy, and summon angels and spirits from the other world. The exact origins and history of the temple are only revealed to third-degree initiates, and much of the information surrounding this fascinating cult has been lost in the mists of time. While in residency at the Last Tuesday Society, the temple will continue to be in regular use when not open to members of the public.

ALCHEMIST'S TOOL BOX
17th century and later
2016, 80 × 25 × 30 cm
Wood, copper, brass, silver, and various organic materials

ALCHEMIST'S TOOL KIT
17th century and later
2016, 14.5 × 12.5 × 46 cm
Wood, copper, brass, silver, and various organic materials

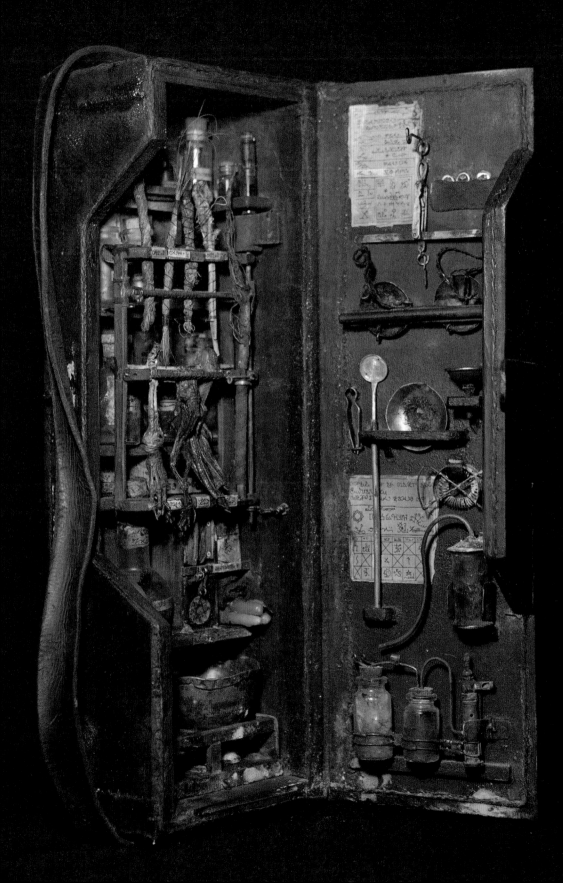

CLARE WINNAN

Clare Winnan is an artist, maker, and upholsterer based in Kent. She is "a reuser of stuff," rescuing landfill, and recycling and revamping things with the sole mission to make them beautiful again. Clare uses these found objects to create pieces that are nostalgic and sometimes kitsch, often summoning childhood memories. When she was little, Clare remembers making dioramas, using objects she had found in her home and garden, such as petals, pebbles—and small dead animals.

This compulsion to make such works has never left Clare; neither has her love of the macabre. Her pieces often have a mischievous twist, in the use of either opposing materials or unlikely media to realize her ideas. Taxidermied animals and the preservation of insects feature heavily in her works, conjuring a sense of the dead coming to life. Like her hands-on approach to fabrics and furniture, there is a tactile, animated dimension to her creations, captured like a vibrant still from a fairytale. Born in Kent, Clare moved to the West Country to study fine art sculpture at Bath Spa University. Her roots drew her back to Kent, however, and she now lives and works in Canterbury with her family.

HANGING ON
2013, 40 × 45 × 15 cm
Wood, chains, paint, dolls house
furniture, chicken skulls

WHITE PHASE
2016, 22 × 15 cm
Dolls house furniture, crab claws,
enamel, and spray paint

CHRIS DRAPER

"I like the democratic nature of what I do," says Chris Draper, "the fact that it's not mysterious and that anyone can have a go . . . all you need is a small hammer and some glue. I can't really claim that the work relies on technical skill or manual dexterity, but I am interested in the decision-making process and how things 'fit' together. Sometimes, using the simplest of objects poses the most difficult decisions. I don't tend to paint, decorate, or fuss too much when I'm making work. Things develop over a period of time and may remain untouched for months until the right elements come together . . . that's the magical moment.

"I collect a *lot* of stuff. In fact, I think I collect collections . . . teeth, Neolithic tools, hands, ex-votos, old photographs, skulls and taxidermy, religious artefacts—the list goes on."

Since his days at art school, Chris has worked extensively as a freelance illustrator, cultivating a unique tactile and textural approach to his much-published practice. Alongside his commissioned work he has been continually involved in education, working from foundation to MA level, and is currently course leader for the illustration degree at the Cambridge School of Art.

SNAKES & LADDERS
2012, 40 × 40 × 6 cm
Original gaming
board, snake skeleton

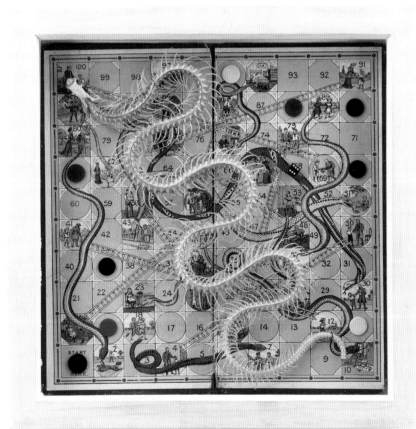

Beyond the world of commissions and education, Chris occasionally works on personal projects, incorporating collage, photography, and three-dimensional constructions, often with minimal intervention. Such projects are based around the theme of nostalgia and "narrative objects," such as lost children's games and fairground rides. "Working with 3D objects requires a commitment to both the objects themselves and a suitable amount of storage space," he explains. "I enjoy working with the imagined stories that the objects I collect and use can tell in different contexts and combinations." Chris's work has been exhibited in the UK, Japan, Ireland, and the Netherlands, and is represented in the personal collection of Sir Peter Blake.

Opposite top left
KING FISHER SOLOIST
2014, 26 × 14 cm
Reconfigured porcelain figures,
glass dome

Opposite bottom left
WAITING FOR DOGGO
2014, 27.5 × 19 cm
Reconfigured porcelain figures,
glass dome

Opposite top right
SAD CLOWN BUDGIE WITH
CONFIDENT STANDING
BUDGIE
2014, 28 × 16 cm
Reconfigured porcelain figures,
glass dome

Above
"BANG" BOX
2012, 40 × 40 × 8 cm
Mixed-media assemblage

JIMMY CAUTY
ADP RIOT TOUR

The *Aftermath Dislocation Principle (ADP)* is an artwork by the English artist and musician Jimmy Cauty. The *ADP* is a 1:87 scale model housed in a 40-foot shipping container. The model is viewed through observation ports in the sides of the container. In 2016, the *ADP* went on a tour of former riot sites across the UK. The following year, the ADP World Riot Tour began, with a mission to visit every historic riot site in the world. Here, we reproduce the artist's own description of the *ADP*.

01. Phase 1 of the *ADP* model took nine months to make with a team of five full-time assistants using traditional model-making materials and kits.
02. Phase 1 was completed in October 2013. It was first exhibited for two weeks in London then toured the Netherlands in 2014.
03. The *ADP* contains approximately three thousand hand-painted British policemen and more emergency vehicles than any real-life policeman has ever seen.
04. Each LED strobe light has been individually programmed so the flashing will always be random and never become synchronized.
05. Everything is at 1:87 scale. Even the sound.
06. Jimmy personally smashed all the windows himself.
07. No one knows what led to this destruction or where all the civilians have gone.
08. Yes, there is a stag on top of one of the high-rise buildings.
09. The *ADP* model was first shown in gallery spaces and railway arches, rather than outside in a shipping container.
10. Back then, the *ADP* was shipped in twenty-three crates and had to be reassembled each time it was exhibited.
11. The *ADP* model was re-engineered as a shipping container–based artwork at the beginning of 2016.
12. To fit the *ADP* model inside the container, 6 inches had to be sawn off its entire length.

13. The *ADP* shipping container is 40 feet long, 8 feet wide and 9½ feet high.
14. The *ADP* now weighs 4½ tonnes and is moved around the world on 30-tonne lorries and container ships.
15. The *ADP* can only be conceived of in imperial units.
16. The *ADP* can be plugged in anywhere and, if no electricity supply is available, it has its own generator.
17. The *ADP* power consumption is 2.5 kilowatts, 240 volts, 16 amperes.

ADP SELFIE AT
DISASTER ZONE
Jimmy Cauty

18. The *ADP* shipping container was originally painted grey with just the *ADP* logos on each side.
19. The graffiti that now covers the container was done by vandals without the control or permission from the artist or *ADP* organizers. When permission has been sought (particularly by those claiming to be artists), it has been denied. The *ADP* policy is that vandalism will be tolerated, but not art.
20. If anyone disagrees with anything written, pictured, or stuck on the container, or finds anything unacceptable or offensive, they must take it upon themselves to change it. The artist and *ADP* organizers cannot and do not take any responsibility for anything written, pictured, or stuck on the container. If they see something they don't like, they may change it. Just as anyone else can.
21. The original ADP Riot Tour started on 23 April 2016 and visited thirty-six riot sites around the UK before Christmas Day 2016.
22. During the 2016 ADP Riot Tour, the container was sometimes left switched on and unattended for days in some of the most hostile areas in the UK. At other times it was switched on and attended for only a few hours per day in shopping centres and suburban gardens.
23. Since its creation in 2013, and by the end of the 2016 ADP Riot Tour, more than 1 million people had seen and born witness to the *ADP*.
24. The last site of the 2016 ADP Riot Tour was at the Panacea Museum in the Garden of Eden. The END TIME was prophesied for 00:23 hours on Christmas Day when all things would end.
25. The 2016 ADP Riot Tour ended on Christmas Day at 00:23 hours but the END TIME—the end of all things—did not happen.
26. Since then, the ADP Riot Tour organizers have had a major rethink and now the ADP Riot Tour will continue. First into Europe and then the rest of the world until the end of time.

27. The *ADP* can only be shown on the site of, or in the context of, a dystopian past or a utopian future.
28. The *ADP* must always be shown for free.
29. The *ADP* is appropriate for small children, old people, and anyone of any age, gender, culture, and sexual/political/religious persuasion. It does, however, contain some swear words, police-on-police violence, and other pleasurable sights. Some parental, socio-political, philosophical, and moral guidance is advised.
30. The *ADP* can be viewed at any time in any weather conditions, but bright sunny days are the enemy of the *ADP*. Optimal viewing conditions are after dark in a hostile urban/suburban/rural environment.
31. No one must ever dictate, pronounce, or try to explain the full meaning of the *ADP*. It can only be seen and discussed, not known.

Opposite top
OBSERVATION
PORT

Opposite centre
ADP ARRIVING
AT THE CHEMIC
TAVERN IN LEEDS

Opposite bottom
ADP EXETER

Top
ADP FOLKESTONE

Above left
ALAN MOORE
SIGNING A
DEDICATION TO
JIMMY CAUTY

Above right
LOCATIONS MAP

Left
RIOT TOUR POSTER

MARCIUS GALAN

The work of the São Paulo–based artist Marcius Galan encompasses sculpture, objects, drawing, and other media, all characterized by a very precise approach to art-making and a particular interest in geometry. In many of his pieces, Marcius carefully reconstructs objects that have been subjected to suppressions or additions, redefining certain aspects of their functionality and form. By intentionally undermining their use-value, Marcius addresses the relationship of these objects with social structures, bureaucratic processes, and economic systems. In its concern with ideas of deceptiveness and frustration, this phenomenological approach has echoes of the Brazilian neo-concrete artists of the 1960s and beyond.

Marcius's eraser drawings are formed by the obsessive action of repeated drawing and rubbing-out. The motifs represented are a circle and a straight line. The paper that is marked by the drawing and the rubbing-out is framed with the residue of the used erasers. The frustrated attempts to build these primary forms tell the story of a drawing that is not actually there. "In this case," explains Marcius, "the drawing is a space between the action and the final work. Both the accumulation of the eraser and the paper that is sculpted by the act of erasing contain the information of this action, which is justified and strengthened through the repetition of error."

Marcius began these works by framing all the residue generated by the erasers he had used for successive drawings over a four-year period. Later, he became more interested in the material itself—in its original form—rather than its remnants. This led to more formal experiments with erasers, in which new or half-used erasers, together with graphite sticks, are arranged in boxes to form immaculate geometric compositions. In relation to the initial drawings, Marcius describes a dematerialization of the drawing process, reduced to the materiality of the tools themselves.

It is interesting to note that the eraser has been used as the main tool in this series, particularly as Marcius is an artist for whom emptiness holds such a fascination. The works effectively extend the notion of the artist as creator of ideas, in the manner of Marcel Duchamp's iconic readymades or Robert Rauschenberg investigating whether an artwork can be produced entirely through erasure.

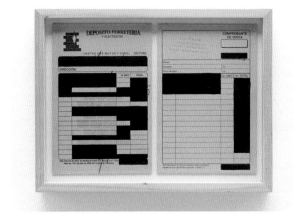

Left
UNTITLED
2014, 17.5 × 24 × 5 cm
Acrylic paint on paper

Opposite top
UNIDA MUNDIAL
2012, 31 × 35 × 5 cm
Erasers on paper

Opposite bottom and pages 236–237
ERASED COMPOSITION
2015, 64 × 92 cm
Rubber erasers on wood

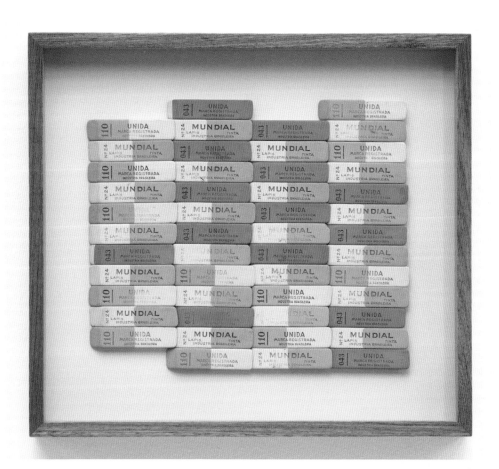

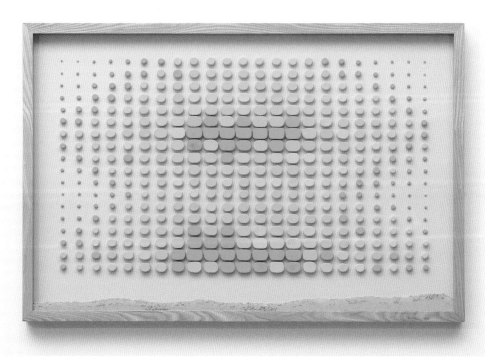

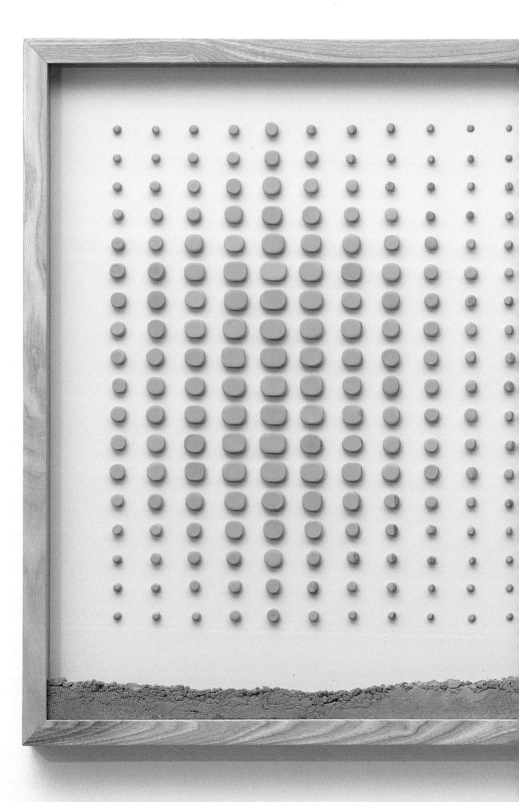

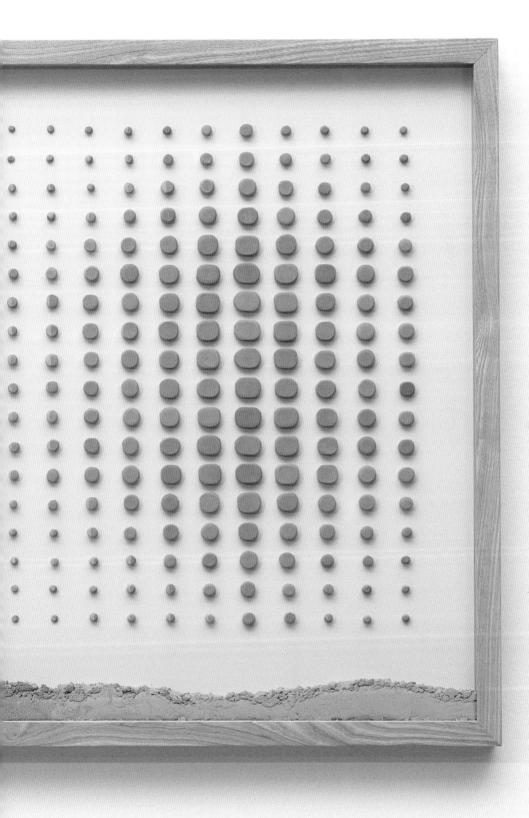

PAOLO GIARDI

Paolo Giardi's project *You Can Learn a Lot of Things From the Flowers* brings to light a forgotten collection of preserved plant specimens that was once assembled by a passionate, amateur botanist. The true identity of this self-taught man remains shrouded in mystery, and all that is known is his enormous appetite for pseudo-scientific research in the natural world. From his studies in ecology, it is possible to trace the foundation of his ideas back to the work of the eighteenth-century Swedish botanist Carl Linnaeus. In his book *Systema Naturae*, Linnaeus set out a revolutionary system of taxonomy based around the number of a flower's reproductive organs, thus recognizing the sexuality of plants. The pollination of stamens and pistils occurring in the secrecy of voluptuous corollas was suddenly seen as mimicking a romantic encounter in some hidden alcove. Botany opened up to the intimacy of sex.

As a late and devoted apostle of Linnaeus's teachings, our inexperienced botanist decided to combine his research on botanical conservation with his passion for *les jeunes filles*, young ladies photographed in seductive poses for the centrefolds of adult publications. The result of this curious obsession is an extensive collection of hybrid creatures, where each playmate is morphed into the nymph Daphne. A herbarium of botanical pin-ups . . .

The title of the series is taken from the lyrics of "All In the Golden Afternoon" from Disney's 1951 *Alice in Wonderland*—specifically, the scene featuring the talking flowers. The project is also a tribute to the wonderful and evocative world created by Marcel Proust in his ode to youth in *À l'Ombre des Jeunes Filles en Fleur* (In the Shadow of Young Girls in Flower), the second volume of *À la Recherche du Temps Perdu*.

Left
PLANT LXIX – ONCIDIUM LAEVE
2014, 28 × 10 cm, Playmen, La Playgirl di Agosto Deidre, paper-cut

Opposite top left
PLANT CLVIII – ZAMIA HORRIDA
2014, 28 × 10 cm, Lui, Joelle, paper-cut

Opposite top right
PLANT LXXXI – CEPHALOTAXUS HARRINGTONIA
2013, 28 × 10 cm, Lui, Irénée, paper-cut

Opposite bottom
PLANT CXXXIII – LASTREA DILATATA
2014, 10 × 28 cm, Playmen, La Playgirl di Marzo, paper-cut

"Since you cannot be my wife, you shall assuredly be my tree. I will wear you for my crown ... And, as eternal youth is mine, you also shall be always green, and your leaf know no decay."
Apollo to Daphne in Ovid's Metamorphoses

For some, the restrictions of the Covid-19 pandemic were a form of solitary confinement; for others, they were an opportunity to explore their obsessions and fantasies. For his inspired lockdown series, *A Room with My View*, Paolo created a series of mock exhibitions—a necessary alternative to the physical space of a gallery, inspired by the current trend of online viewing rooms (OVRs). Pushing the concept a little further, Paolo's series subverts the boundaries of OVRs and what is recognizable as an official presentation of art, adopting the role of art curator. As everything is already set as a virtual stage, asked Paolo, why not make that imaginary platform the final outcome? In this ongoing study, venues and specific rooms are selected in the context of the work on display. The connection between Marcel Proust's bedroom and *You Can Learn a Lot of Things From the Flowers* is an obvious one, given that Proust's writings helped inspire the series. Sigmund Freud's studio, meanwhile, has become the

setting for a group show that includes various artists alongside pieces from Paolo's series *Flora Chimera*, in a personal adaptation of Freud's *Interpretation of Dreams*.

A Room With My View is both a virtual and a physical space, a three-dimensional collage in miniature of carefully curated shows. The process of documentation blends the two realities together, making the simulation come to life.

Opposite top
MARCEL PROUST'S
BEDROOM, MUSÉE
CARNAVALET,
PARIS
2020, cardboard,
foam board, paper,
magazine print, inkjet
print, laser print, oil on
paper, image transfer
film, fabric

This page
Selection of works
from FLORA
CHIMERA (detail
opposite bottom)
2019–2020, 40.5 × 81 ×
5 cm, 81 × 40.5 × 5 cm
Cut-out vintage
magazine centerfolds,
insect pins, color-
aid matt paper in
handmade box

ALEXANDER KORZER-ROBINSON

Alexander Korzer-Robinson is a maker of exquisite paper constructions, finely hollowed out of 150-year-old Victorian books. For his source material, Alexander uses only the illustrations in the books themselves; the end result is like a stage set, or a layered composition similar to the paper theatres that were hugely popular in the nineteenth century. After adding a protective cover, the books are then sealed, to be hung on a wall or enjoyed as a stand-alone piece of art.

Through the tradition of collage, Alexander is pursuing a personal interest in creating small-scale narrative scenes. By making use of antiquarian books, the works are simultaneously an exploration and a

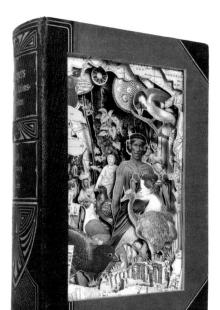

deconstruction of nostalgia. "By using pre-existing media as a starting point," explains the artist, "certain boundaries are set by the material, which I aim to transform through my process. Thus, an encyclopedia can become a window into an alternate world, much like lived reality becomes its alternate in remembered experience. These books, having been stripped of their utilitarian value by the passage of time, regain new purpose. They are no longer tools to learn about the world, but rather a means to gain insight about oneself."

While highly regarded for his book sculptures, Alexander also makes shadow boxes. One of these works, *Swarm 2020: A Souvenir of the Plague Year*, proved a highlight at the 2020 Royal Academy Summer Exhibition in London. A nineteenth-century lady is wearing a modern-day Covid-19 mask, surrounded by a kaleidoscopic rainbow of butterflies, all presented as a diorama. This magical, *Alice in Wonderland*–like freeze seemed to capture a universal mood, with all 150 editions finding a buyer.

VÖGEL DER WELT
1963, 34 × 26 × 4 cm
Newly cut antiquarian book sculpture

MEYERS 19
1906, 35 × 14 × 7 cm
Newly cut antiquarian book sculpture

ZUR GUTEN STUNDE
1897, 31 × 24 × 3.5 cm
Newly cut antiquarian book sculpture

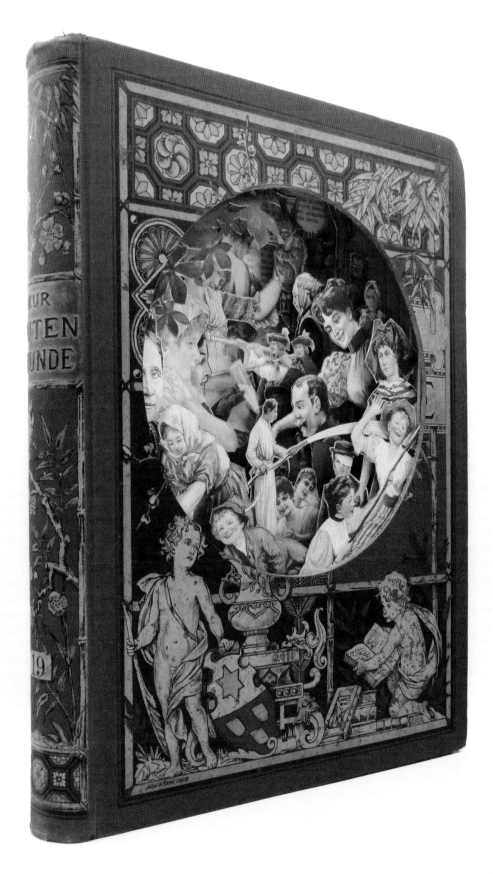

JAY ROSS

Jay Ross's *Empty Signs* is an anthropological collection of photographs of blank, broken, and otherwise empty American signs. The process of documenting the signs began in Albuquerque, New Mexico, in 2012 and continues to this day, capturing signage in Louisville, Kentucky; Michigan; San Antonio, Texas; and predominantly Columbus, Ohio, where Jay currently resides.

The project asks as many questions as it provides answers, if not more. Are the signs a romantic road map of the American dream, or are they rusted symbols of a "boom and bust" economy? Either way, there is an innate beauty to these vacant vessels, one that could tell many stories. Among other things, they bring to mind Julien Temple's film *Requiem for Detroit?* (2010), in which he describes the near-deserted metropolis of the film's title as fast becoming the first "post-American city." Artist and documentarian Lowell Boileau describes the recent history of the Motor City as "a slow-motion Katrina." Yet despite the aftermath of bankruptcy, disintegrating industries, and of course Covid-19, young people are helping the city to live again.

For his part, Lowell started *The Fabulous Ruins of Detroit*, a website that offered an admiring take on the city's crumbling architecture, and which gave birth to the inspirational online community forum *Detroit Yes!*. "The rediscovery of Detroit by suburban kids was emerging," said Boileau. "They were asking how they could live in Detroit and how they could be part of the solution. People were trying to make sense of Detroit." Ross's empty signs are universal remnants of a rich past of promise

and production. Perhaps they represent voids to be filled with hope, an exhilarating opportunity to start over, a pioneer's map to a post-industrial future that might await us all.

In addition to photographing signs, Jay works at Case Western Reserve University in Cleveland, Ohio. His interests include the overlap between creativity, community, education, and social justice. Another of his projects is called *Displaced Shopping Carts*.

Left, opposite, and pages 246–247
EMPTY SIGNS
Selected works, 2012–2021

BRYAN BENGE

In the words of German philosopher Walter Benjamin, "The work of memory collapses time." Bryan Benge draws on autobiography, family history, and cultural icons from his past to explore visual memory and a re-positioning of the forgotten. Memory is not an instrument for surveying the past, but its theatre. Benge mirrors the language of gaming technology, referring back to such early examples of Pop art as the *Bunk* series of collages made by Eduardo Paolozzi in the late 1940s. He is also interested in the recovery of early memories and the impact of loss and bereavement.

First seen in maquette form, Bryan's *Car Shack* was exhibited at the James Hockey Gallery at UCA Farnham in Surrey. Composed of, literally, a car and a shack, the work was a synthesis of the manufactured and the "handfactured." The shack is a primal shelter, a sign for home. It possess the mantle of poverty and, as destitution increases, it gives us access to absolute refuge. The car is redolent of power and freedom, yet we now find ourselves hostage to its lust for resources. In Bryan's work, it has become a monument to the space where we become enraged, retreat into personal habits, make love, and die.

As well as a practising artist, Bryan is a senior lecturer in art and design. He is also an active member of such art collectives as the London Group, Collect Connect, and Group East.

CAR SHACK (MAQUETTE)
2012, 45 × 36 × 25 cm
Wood and painted sculpture in Perspex box

Car Shack *at the James Hockey Gallery,*
UCA Farnham, Surrey

PAUL BURGESS

Having worked at the same illustration agency as the author in the 1990s, Paul Burgess is now a principal lecturer at the University of Brighton. In addition to producing commissions, Burgess has exhibited his collage-based artworks in numerous exhibitions around the UK and abroad. He is the co-author of *Satellite: Sex Pistols – Memorabilia, Locations, Photography, Fashion* and a regular contributor to various music and design publications.

Paul's research interests include contemporary collage, graphics related to sound, and music in popular culture. He is especially interested in the opportunities afforded by errors within illustration and graphic design. In addition, he is an avid collector of found ephemera and a keen champion of self-publishing. His fascination with amateur and outsider art extends to the work of such artists as Ken Woodward.

LONDON LOVES
2014, 60 × 60 × 40 cm
Collage and print assemblage

A

4

I

R

DANIEL AGDAG
MISCELLANEOUS ASSEMBLIES

"The conception of using cardboard first arose from necessity. I found it was a medium that was easy to acquire and manipulate using simple hand tools to form my ideas. For me, the narrower the medium, the broader my ideas become. This limitation allows me to be limitlessly imaginative with it. And for me, it is fluid to work with—without the need for elaborate tools and a large dedicated space. That said, I am constantly surprised by the limits to which I can take it. The most important thing about it is that, as a medium, for me it offers the least amount of resistance to conceive and express my ideas."

Daniel Agdag is an artist, sculptor, and animator based in Melbourne, Australia. He describes his practice as "sketching with cardboard." Using only boxboard (a thin type of cardboard), glue, and a scalpel, he is able to create extremely intricate universes. Intentionally keeping his working methods very simple—but the outcome very complex—he works intuitively by hand without detailed plans or drawings. There is no attempt, either, to conceal the raw materials of his microworlds. The boxboard, he says, lends his sculptures and sets "a romantic, sepia-filled, glowy aspect." Indeed, their monochromatic nature allows the viewer to hone in on the striking and beautiful detail of their construction.

Daniel, who says he wants to "make order out of chaos," spends a lot of time in the urban environment, observing and absorbing the man-made world. He is trying, he says, to bring the beauty of it to people's attention. "Look at these complex systems. They allow you to have a life, they allow you to live in a very complex civilization where you are able to participate in things that you might never have been able to [be involved in] without the introduction of these machines and these technologies."

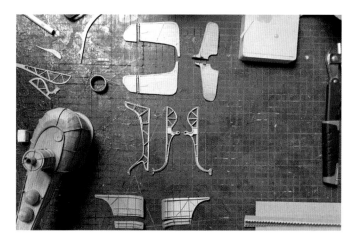

Page 251
THE 2ND COMPARTMENT
2019, 58.5 × 30.5 × 30.5 cm
Cardboard, trace paper,
mounted on timber base with
hand-blown glass dome

CONSTRUCTION WORK

SETS FOR A FILM I'LL NEVER
MAKE (detail)
2012–2016, dimensions variable
Cardboard, trace paper,
electronics

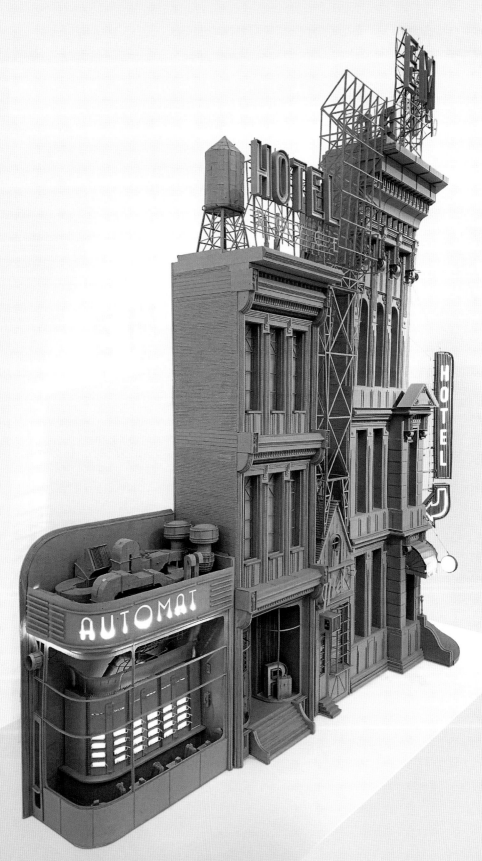

Daniel's exquisite machines whir and hum with imagined kinetic energy, as if about to burst into life. Immediately catching and holding one's attention, they also follow an internal logic, where every crank, pulley, and cog has a functioning role. In his recent series *Radio Silence*, there is a sense of something being transmitted, but with an absence of sound. All his pieces display a remarkable technological sophistication.

During the Covid-19 pandemic, Daniel moved his "studio" to his one-bedroom apartment in Melbourne. Working in lockdown allowed him to pull out a scalpel in the middle of the night and continue shaping one of his creations. "I don't start off with an idea of the full piece in its entirety," he explains. "It's always in flux; everything is on the fly; nothing is set in stone at any point throughout the process." His 9-minute film, *The Lost Property Office*, is a meticulously handcrafted stop-motion animation. The art deco, post–industrial world depicted in the film was fashioned over a period of 18 months using 2,500 sheets of recycled cardboard, all patiently hand-cut using 1,287 scalpel blades to create 1,258 elaborate set pieces and individual props. Produced with Liz Kearney, the film was nominated for an Academy Award in 2018.

MACHINE/INSTRUMENT No. 2
2018, 65 × 30.5 × 30.5 cm
Boxboard, paper, Hermle carriage
movement, mounted on Victorian
ash base, under low-iron glass vitrine

THE MINOR INSTALLATION
2020, 58.5 × 30.5 × 30.5 cm
Cardboard, trace paper,
mounted on timber base with
hand-blown glass dome

THE GENERAL &
THE CABOOSE
2017, 58.5 × 30.5 × 30.5 cm
Cardboard, trace paper,
mounted on timber base with
hand-blown glass dome

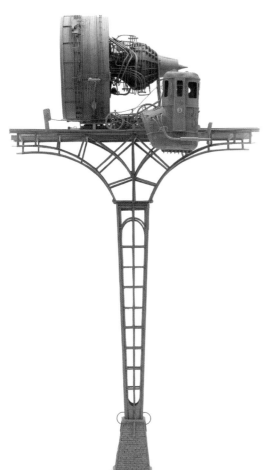

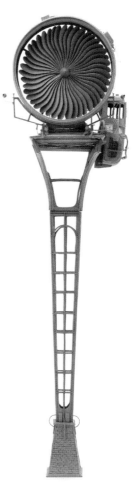

BENJAMIN SHINE

Artist and designer Benjamin Shine is widely known for his pioneering *Flow* series featuring ethereal depictions of a woman's face made from a single stretch of tulle. The artist uses the tulle in bright, coloured hues to craft intricate portraits of meditative expression, contemplating impermanence and the relationship between the spiritual and the superficial. His work has been exhibited extensively, from the Metropolitan Museum of Art in New York to the Design Museum in London.

Benjamin is a multidisciplinary artist and designer dedicated to bringing new ideas into existence, in the areas of fashion, furniture, and product design. Originally created as a one-off piece for the 2012 *BT Art Box* exhibition in aid of the children's charity Child Line, *Box Lounger* moves the iconic British telephone box indoors, transformed into a functional piece of furniture. Featuring button-back red-leather upholstery and an illuminated "Telephone" sign, *Box Lounger* packs a patriotic punch in its fusion of British heritage design. The inspiration for *Analog Sidetable* came from reports of old analogue television sets being dumped on the street to make way for the digital changeover in 2012. The retro design was intended to convert the classic 1960s TV into a fresh and purposeful piece while also shining a spotlight on its origins—which might otherwise be easily forgotten.

BOX LOUNGER
2012, 82 × 220 × 90 cm
Customized telephone box, fibreglass, and leather upholstery

ANALOG SIDETABLE
2011, 60 × 35 × 45 cm
Upcyled television, stainless steel, and mirror

LOVE HULTÉN

Swedish audiovisual artist and craftsman Love Hultén uses traditional craftsmanship and modern technology to create unique objects in an unexpected merging of form and function. "I used to tear electronic toys apart, trying to understand their insides," he says, finding his true calling in the woodshop. Hultén combines fine woodcraft and hand-wired electronics to produce musical works of art. His creations include expressive and tactile synthesizers, retro-inspired games consoles, and other, truly funky audiovisual contraptions that bring together the organic and the electronic.

Love's "Brix System" pays homage to the world's most famous construction toy with a deluxe suite of 6:1 scale models of Lego bricks. "I want my objects to create a state of curiosity, not just nostalgia," he explains. "Nostalgia is involved to a certain extent, yes, but not by looking backwards. It's by taking steps in different directions simultaneously by using fragments from both the past and the present, creating unique and balanced objects." Specializing in exclusive, one-of-a-kind items, he offers the client a genuine and personal experience. Everything is crafted, polished, and assembled by Hultén in his one-man studio located in Gothenburg, Sweden.

Top
VOC-25
2020, 55 × 40 × 40 cm
Wood, plastic teeth, and electronics

Left and bottom
BRIX SYSTEM
A series of handcrafted wooden electronic devices inspired by Lego, including telephones and music-making devices

Opposite
TRIACCORD
2018, 30 × 20 × 3 cm
Wood and electronics
A theramin-like device from a three-part installation on sight, hearing, and touch

DRUMMOND + HAMMETT

From a small workshop in the heart of Bristol, Pat Hammett makes "cigar-box guitars"—unique, handmade stringed instruments that are steeped in tradition, and which are quirky and enjoyable to play. The concept of using home-made instruments can be traced back to the pioneers of the blues, founded in the rural southern states of America during a time of hardship, economic depression, and racial segregation. Among these pioneers was Blind Willie Johnson, Charlie Patton, Muddy Waters, Howlin' Wolf, and Son House, leading to the likes of Lightnin' Hopkins, Jimi Hendrix, Hound Dog Taylor, Big Bill Broonzy, and Junior Kimbrough. Today, the cigar-box tradition is kept alive by such musicians as Sea Sick Steve, Reverend Peyton, and Jack White.

Cigar-box guitars require a stripped-back playing style and encourage open tunings. Pat was attracted to them by the crudeness of their rudimentary design; for his own creations, he experiments with different boxes and the varying resonance of different timbers. According to Pat, no two cigar-box guitars are alike. Sadly, the making of such guitars is a vanishing art— hopefully to be revived by all those twangers who picked up a guitar during lockdown.

Opposite
ESPECIAL
Vintage cigar box with graphic label of choice (see below), Waverley-style "New Age" tuning pegs, ornate corner pieces, mother-of-pearl fret markers, 17-fret black walnut finger board, solid maple neck, mahogany body, through-string tail-end ferrules, Gibson-style headstock with 1920s nickel coin inset, 24¾-inch fret scale, rosewood bridge, solid-bone nut, and a mini-humbucker with volume control and chrome control knob

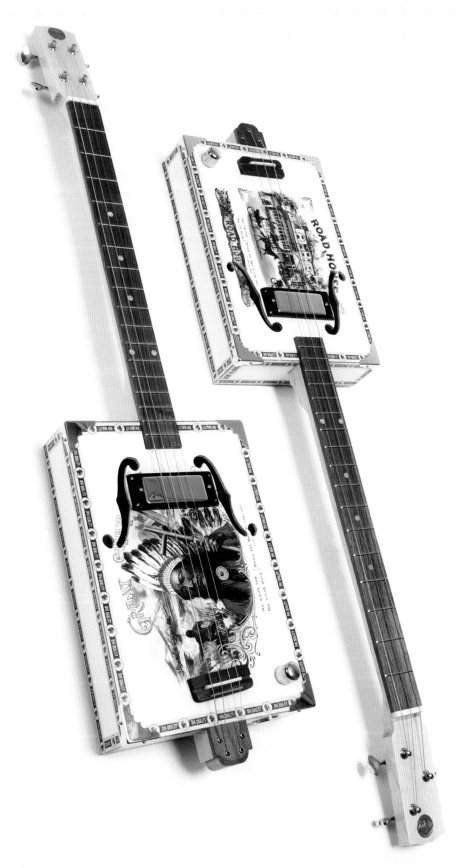

THE INSECT CIRCUS MUSEUM

"Ladies & Gentlemen. Boys & Girls. Stroll Up, Stroll Up for the Magnificent Insect Circus Museum! Behold the Liberty Beetles & the Cheeky Ladybirds! Be thrilled by the Knife Thrower & the Painted Lady! Gasp as Captain Courage, the intrepid Wasp Tamer, defies Danger! Marvel at the Worm Charmer & laugh at the Dancing Snails!"

Edinburgh has suggested it might just be the best thing ever in the whole wide world, while reports in Suffolk claim it is a grin-inducing treat, not just for the children you know, but also for your own inner child . . . Housed in a vintage, mahogany-lined Bedford TK beetlebox lorry, this unique museum displays a stunning array of costumes, props, puppets, toys, and ephemera from the extraordinary collection of the Insect Circus Society.

Spanning more than three centuries, and covering many continents, this is undeniably the finest museum of its kind. Of special attraction are dioramas and push-button mechanical peep-show models depicting scenes from the famous Piper family insect circus. Featuring such perennial favourites as dancing snails, trained butterflies, wasp tamers, and balancing bugs, these stunning automata are a rare treat for all ages. If you are interested in having the Insect Circus Museum and Mechanical Menagerie pay a visit to your town or event, says the literature, then please do not hesitate to contact the museum administrator, Ronald McPeak, for terms and conditions. It also states that insect cruelty is certainly not tolerated by the museum, and that it is regularly inspected by the RSPCI . . .

INSECT CIRCUS MUSEUM
ON LOCATION

RARE INTERIOR VIEW OF
MUSEUM, INCLUDING PEEP-
HOLE DIORAMAS

A SELECTION OF ORIGINAL
POSTERS FROM 1880 TO 1927

Zazelle!
Le Lanceur de Couteau

Natif de Marseille

Cirque des Insectes
252 RUE S'HONORÉ. Tous les Soirs À 8ʜ½
PRIX des PLACES: LOGE 5ꜰˢ FAUTEUIL 3ꜰˢ GALERIE 2ꜰˢ

Imp. & dessins Lionel Lévy, 35 Rue des Petits-Champs, Paris.

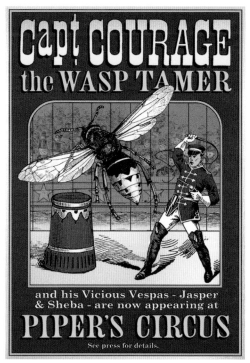

Capt COURAGE
the **WASP TAMER**

and his Vicious Vespas - Jasper
& Sheba - are now appearing at
PIPER'S CIRCUS
See press for details.

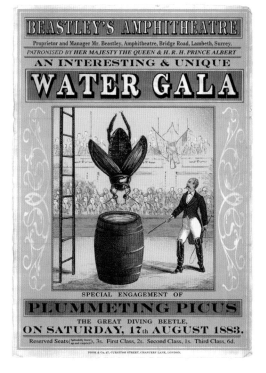

BEASTLEY'S AMPHITHEATRE.
Proprietor and Manager Mr. Beastley, Amphitheatre, Bridge Road, Lambeth, Surrey.
PATRONISED BY HER MAJESTY THE QUEEN & H. R. H. PRINCE ALBERT
AN INTERESTING & UNIQUE
WATER GALA

SPECIAL ENGAGEMENT OF
PLUMMETING PICUS
THE GREAT DIVING BEETLE,
ON SATURDAY, 17th AUGUST, 1883.
Reserved Seats (splendidly lined up and carpeted), 3s. First Class, 2s. Second Class, 1s. Third Class, 6d.

POOK & Co. 27, CURSITOR STREET, CHANCERY LANE, LONDON.

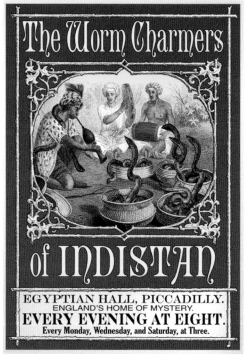

The Worm Charmers
of INDISTAN

EGYPTIAN HALL, PICCADILLY.
ENGLAND'S HOME OF MYSTERY.
EVERY EVENING AT EIGHT.
Every Monday, Wednesday, and Saturday, at Three.

TOM SANDERSON

"Have nothing in your house that you do not know to be useful, or believe to be beautiful."
William Morris

Morris's wise words sum up Tom Sanderson's love of objects, living his life as an artisan-craftsman the old-fashioned way with his family in the heart of Sussex. In 2015 Tom set up the Hawkmoth Leather Company, working on his own to produce unique handcrafted leather goods. Created using traditional methods and materials, from the edging and burnishing to the meticulous wax-thread stitching and multiple layers of dye, Tom's products are made to last a lifetime.

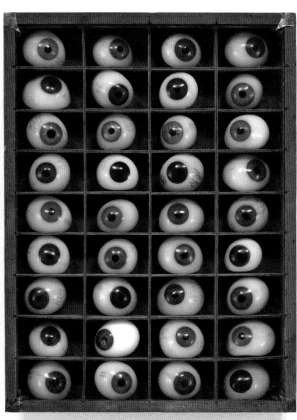

Tom has a rich background in film, folk music, and gardening. Of particular importance to his practice are the lost traditions of a bygone era of small-scale production, when quality, craftsmanship, and longevity were paramount. Inspired by history and the eclectic weave of British culture, Tom restores a rustic beauty to the discarded.

Ever since he was a child, Tom has been drawn to the weird and wonderful. Of *The Eyes Have It*, he says: "I saw these Victorian eyes in a Cornish shop window. I knew I had to have them. As soon as I got them home I wanted to see if I could express their individual characters artistically, directly, and humorously. Some cork, a box of glass, and the eyes came alive." The playful "ayes" of the work's title means "yeses," imbuing Tom's little eyeball collective with a pleasing positivity.

THE AYES HAVE IT
2010, 19 × 15 × 5cm
Victorian glass eyes, type case, glass

TOM BUCHANAN

"Objects are my dictionary . . . useless things. People see it as clusters of junk. I see it as clusters of possibility. Each object is a line. It gives direction, picked up here and things there, indeed gleaned. I make a sentence of things whose shapes at first are very simple and seem the same but whose variations are infinite." *Louis Pons*

Sometimes I think music has too much significance in my life. I am like a sonic radar; my ears prick up at the first sign of new sounds. My whole being and existence can be archived into some kind of sensory library. This is exactly how I define my relationship to objects: it is a second sense. I might not remember what I did yesterday, but I may have just found an item that has changed my life forever, just like a song. It is the possibility and curiosity of these things that are my lifeblood, a compulsive urgency to keep searching.

     I honestly wonder if the find is half the journey; the greater the circumstances of the discovery, the more it might be cherished. As the Louis Pons quotation suggests, being able to see the possibility in objects is a form of visual literacy. To use the metaphor of music one last time, I remember something a music journalist once said: "People change, but records don't, and that's part of what makes them great. They're frozen in place, ready to be found by people who need them. And if you haven't found these yet—well, I'm jealous."

SEVEN
DEADLY SINS
2015, 34 × 34 × 13 cm
Tupperware lids, glass
amber lamp lens in
wooden box frame

For many years I worked as a freelance illustrator, increasingly making my commissions more playful. *Pegman* was one of those landmark pieces, created with the help of my brother, who I photographed swinging from some scaffolding. I have a bold affinity with graphics, and love the restless creativity of the likes of Barney Bubbles and the hands-on experimentation of such artists as Tomasz Boguslawski.

I once described one of my box works as a suspended pinball machine, likening the concept to freeze-framing something in perpetual motion. The box frame allows you to enhance a story very effectively—as well as helping you to know when to stop. My latest project is re-animating discarded plates, using them as random stage sets. In the words of Tom Waits, "We have a deficit of wonder right now." If only we could just forget about our phones, be present long enough to delve a little deeper.

I have always been interested in process, in the mechanics of cause and effect. Sometimes I despair that we are losing touch with tactile curiosity, a very unique kind of magic and awe. Take the theatre production of Michael Morpurgo's *War Horse*—made with the Handspring Puppet Company—and compare it to Steven Spielberg's Hollywood blockbuster: each belongs to a totally different realm of experience.

RED MIST
2020, 35 × 35 × 5 cm
Illustrated ceramic plate in
wooden tinted box frame

PERILOUS GAME
OF PEGMAN
2002, 57 × 40.6 × 7 cm
Mixed-media assemblage,
photographs/prints on nails

It is sobering to think that, in a single lifetime, you can witness the fall of one historic wall only for another to be erected and divide an entire continent. The last time a country tried to separate itself completely from its neighbour was in Berlin in 1961. John Wayne, the true Marlboro Man, personified the frontier heritage of the United States. Wayne starred in 142 films, playing outlaws, cavalrymen, and unconquerable loners in 83 of them, keeping the American dream alive. Throughout most of his life, he was a prominent conservative Republican, supporting anti-communist policies. In 1968, at the height of America's involvement in Vietnam, Wayne directed and starred in *The Green Berets*, driven by the growing anti-war movement in his own country. Many critics described the film as absurdist, cliched propaganda, as real a depiction of conflict as a game of "Cowboys and Indians." In an infamous 1971 *Playboy* interview, Wayne was still expressing his support for Vietnam, prompting a firestorm of headlines over comments about social issues and race relations.

Today, such talk of white supremacy and the power of celebrity sounds frighteningly familiar. During his time as the highest-profile Republican star in Hollywood, party backers asked if he might run for national office. Wayne declined, joking that he could never believe the public would accept an actor in the White House. Ronald Reagan aside, you have to contemplate the extraordinary unfolding story of Ukrainian president Volodymyr Zelenskyy.

MARTIAL LAW
2016, 70 × 38 × 25 cm
Mixed-media assemblage

PETER QUINNELL
THE COLLECTOR COLLECTOR

Peter Quinnell has been working with collage and assemblage for more than thirty years, building up a vast collection of images and objects. As his website states: "Experienced, flexible, fast and inexpensive; no job too large or small." After studying at Chelsea College of Arts and the Royal College of Art in London, Peter became a renowned illustrator, collaborating with another artist, Magda Archer, from 1984 to 1999 as the pioneering collage duo Archer/Quinnell. Peter's work has appeared in magazines, on book jackets, on record sleeves, in shop windows, and as part of advertising campaigns in the UK and internationally.

In the seaside town of Hastings, East Sussex, Peter's reputation precedes him. In the "Jack in the Green" parade celebrating May Day, hearty locals dressed as bunters, chimney sweeps, and milkmaids follow the Morris-dancing druids through the streets of the Old Town. There's always one person in the parade who stands out, and on one occasion it was Peter, dressed as a large beaked crow peddling a tricycle, adorned from head to toe in badges, glistening like a pagan Pearly King.

PQ ON HASTINGS SEAFRONT

SQUATTERS
2007, 19 × 41 × 14 cm
Mixed-media assemblage

THE PIECE OF COD
THAT SURPASSETH ALL
UNDERSTANDING
2012, 38 × 38 × 12 cm
Mixed-media assemblage

Pages 272–273
I'M LOVIN' IT
2013, 18 × 42 × 11 cm
Mixed-media assemblage

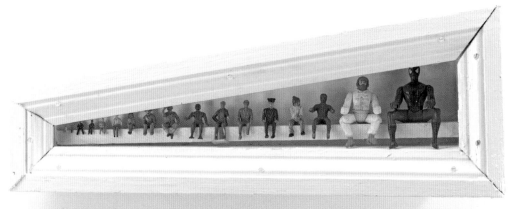

"It's not about completing the set, it's more about having the raw material to work with, to create the perfect picture. I have always collected stuff, but mainly not in specific categories, just all sorts of detritus that attracts me. The use of the real objects in my work is an excuse for the collecting. It's probably some sort of mental illness." *Peter Quinnell*

Often to be seen at local car boot sales, Peter regularly exhibits his art, as well as teaching at University Centre Hastings and running local projects. It is said that his children's workshops are so popular that some attendees refused to leave once they had outgrown the classes. Peter and his illustrator partner, Claire Fletcher, share the eclectic Black Winkle studio, next to the funicular railway and fishing huts in Rock-a-Nore, an area of Hastings. They are both actively involved in community arts programmes, while Claire runs Made in Hastings, a shop celebrating locally sourced art.

Peter is a member of Radiator Arts, one of whose projects was *Hermit: A Life on the Margins*, an installation of animation and sound exploring the life and times of John Hancox, a loner who lived in Ecclesbourne Glen cave for around fourteen years until his death in 1904. John was a professional draper who fell on hard times and ended up making a home for himself in the cave, tending his allotment while scraping a living as a "market gardener," as recorded in the 1901 census. Regarded by the locals as a solitary, well-presented, peaceful man who would sing to himself in the woods, John's story remains highly relevant. The project examined themes around homelessness and a life on the edge of society. Using art materials and found objects, participants were moved to make their own spaces—real and illusory worlds within boxes exploring the idea of "a place of one's own." A collaboration between Radiator Arts and local charity Seaview, *Hermit* showed how creativity can make a real difference to people's happiness and general well-being.

There is an infectious, life-affirming immediacy to Peter's creative urges. Even the delivery of his artworks to the *Out of the Box* exhibitions proved refreshing. Rather than china wrapped in reams of protective bubble wrap, there were all these jagged boxes, unceremoniously piled into two large crates. The first show happened to be in the premises

of a number of art studios, one of which was occupied by a most refined joiner who was quite perturbed by the ramshackle nature of Peter's exhibits. They simply could not comprehend the nail gun–scarred, dazzle-daubed nature of the woodwork; by the end of the event, however, they had completely fallen under Peter's spell. The humour expressed in Peter's work inspired the title of this feature. "The Collector Collector" is actually the title of a book by British novelist Tibor Fischer. The narrator of the tale (and the collector of its collectors) is an ancient Mesopotamian bowl, which finds itself in the south London flat of its new owner, Rosa. The bowl not only acts as a repository for 5,000 years of human history, but also is able to communicate with those who handle it, reading memories and imparting wisdom. One wonders if Peter has such a magic gift with the inanimate.

Opposite top
LIGHT BOXES
2019, various sizes
Mixed media and electronics

Opposite bottom
CHICKEN CHOKIN' JESUS
2012, 22 × 13 × 9 cm
Mixed-media assemblage

Right
MADONNA & CHILD
2012, 26 × 15 × 12 cm
Mixed-media assemblage

Below
HUEVOS RANCHEROS
2009, 35 × 35 × 10 cm
Mixed-media assemblage

Pages 276–277
LITTLE BLUE FOLKS
2011, 20 × 72 × 16 cm
Mixed-media assemblage

YRJÖ EDELMANN

Yrjö Edelmann was a celebrated Swedish painter. With a background in comic strips and illustration, he is best known for his hyperrealist depictions of clumsily wrapped packages and boxes. "One day in 1976," he explained, "I looked out of the window in my studio and saw just this one single cloud. If I'd just painted that, it would've just been an ordinary landscape painting, and I didn't want that. But then I suddenly noticed a piece of crinkled paper on my table, and so I cut it to the shape of a cloud, and painted that against a realistic landscape." So began his experiments with *trompe l'oeil*, masterfully blending thin layers of oil paint using a traditional Renaissance glazing technique.

By only depicting wrapped parcels, Yrjö maintained a convincing sense of tension and mystery in his work, making you wonder what might actually be underneath all that wrapping paper. You cannot help but be fascinated by the shady depths of these crumpled shapes, not to mention the dedication required to make them. Whether they are works of reality or fantasy, the viewer becomes swept up in a dreamy seascape of almost infinite proportions. This selection of Yrjö's paintings has been reproduced with the kind permission of Galleri GKM, which exclusively represents the artist's estate.

WRAPPED SUNNY
LANDSCAPE II
1999, 80 × 65 × 4 cm
Oil on canvas

NOW CONSIDER
WHAT IS NECESSARY
2015, 61 × 87 × 4 cm
Oil on canvas

A PACKED VIEW OVER
HARMONIC BLUE FIELDS
2011, 90 × 80 × 4 cm
Oil on canvas

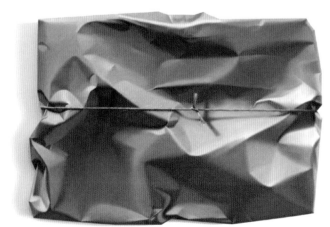

LUCIA HARLEY

"Empires are built and crumble, people are born and die, an onward flow of atoms that cannot be halted, however much we like to think we are in control. It's dynamic, sometimes frightening, but always something to be embraced."

Lucia Harley is fascinated by the state of flux in which life exists. Based in Somerset, England, Lucia runs immersive workshops, curating educational programmes through creativity. Her own work delves beneath the surface of day-to-day ritual, exploring the entanglement of thought, memory, and emotion. She has spent a significant amount of time in Brazil, where she has family, and where she studied at the University of São Paulo. Her father is a botanist who, for many years, worked at the Royal Botanic Gardens, Kew, where his collection of plants is housed within the herbarium.

Working on location, Lucia creates intuitive installations and interventions using objects and mixed media to explore the space in which they are made, creating opportunities for reflection. Her practice is concerned with capturing the fleeting, transient moments of life, distilling them into art forms, including performance. As a site-specific artist, working within the confines of a box was not something that came naturally; it took a shift in perspective to see the box as just another space with which to engage, like any other environment.

According to Lucia, *Dia Noite* (which translates from the Portuguese as "Day Night") is based on the concept of flux, akin to one of the kinetic sculptures she often makes with children. Within *This Time Is Real*, a miniature universe is created. A child looks out into a seeming expanse of nothingness, surrounded by the sands of time; on the adjacent panel, trajectories and pathways overlap one another, coloured threads sewn into the silk. The notion of physical action as outcome, such as the marks and patterns created by the moving body, is an important aspect of Lucia's work.

Plateau captures a moment of uncertainty, a stop, the unconnected pieces of a puzzle. No one else probably even notices this moment, a blip that makes us human.

PLATEAU
2012, 15 × 25 × 1.5 cm
Mixed media in customized box

DIA NOITE
2014, 80 × 18 × 35 cm
Mixed-media assemblage, science lab detritus

THIS TIME IS REAL
2014, 15 × 25 × 1.5 cm
Mixed media in customized box

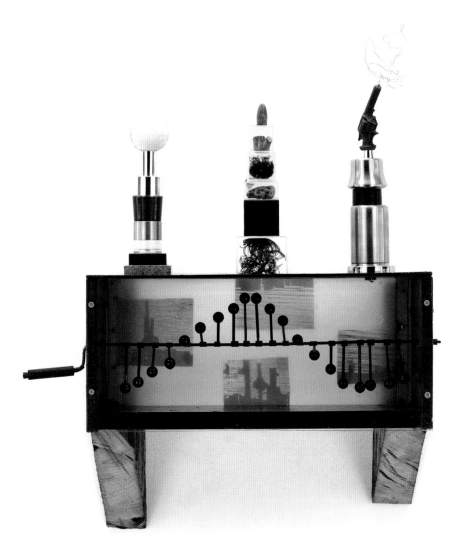

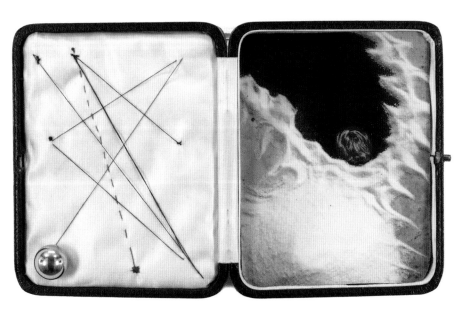

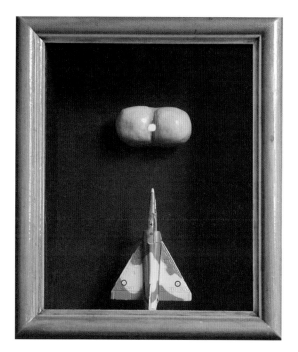

ZUZUSHII ART LABORATORY

ZUZUSHII ART LABORATORY is a multidimensional arts partnership composed of Fumico Azuma and Tim Can, whose creative paths first overlapped in Barcelona in 1999. In addition to working in the Catalan capital, they have set up camp in their respective home cities of Tokyo and London, not to mention Bali, Berlin, and the Greek island of Naxos. Indeed, their projects have taken them around the world, to such diverse places as Lapland, Eastern Europe, and Taiwan. Working mainly together, they also operate as individuals, focused on their own particular concerns.

Fumico and Tim's approach to producing art is highly utilitarian, encompassing installation, film, photography, sound, and performance (as ZUZUSHII MONKEY), as well as creative writing, collage, and assemblage. Their geographically opposed backgrounds and the detritus of their somewhat nomadic lifestyles have given birth to many interests and concerns along the way, such as ecology, minimalism, probing the unlit corners of human experience, and playing with the absurd, profound, and ominously dark.

Looking into the self-restricted world of a ZUZUSHII box offers a glimmer of a greater story, of staged allegories with a conscience. One sees grand scenarios in miniature, shadows of things to come, or perhaps even tangible evidence of unreal worlds. Among other metaphysical diversions, Fumico finds inspiration in the concept of "nothingness"; Tim, meanwhile, feels and plays with the raw energy held within objects. The results can be atmospheric memories, reflections from life, visions with possible warnings, cynicism caught behind glass. Their laboratory is currently based in Hastings on the south coast of England, where they are busy preparing for their next voyage.

HOLE
2016, 28 × 21 × 8 cm
*Mixed media, toy aircraft,
clay, electronics*
Fumico Azuma

HOW DO WE HEAR?
2018, 30 × 12 × 10 cm
*Mixed media, photo, found
chains, paint*
Tim Can

6th FINGER
2016, 30 × 30 × 10 cm
*Handwritten calligraphy,
photos, found objects*
Fumico Azuma

LET'S PLAY
2015, 22 × 15 × 10 cm
Mixed media, found objects
Tim Can

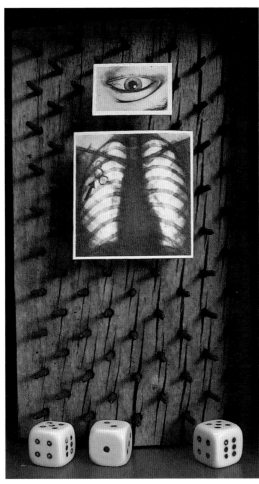

HITESH NATALWALA

Born in Africa to parents of Indian descent, brought up in England, and now living in Spain after spending twelve years in Australia, Hitesh Natalwala brings a plethora of cultural influences to his art, defining his own personal iconography. Hitesh uses his love of found materials to breathe life into moments, experiences, and emotions from a past that lives only in the collective memory of those involved and, at this stage of his life, of some who are no longer alive.

Hitesh is an avid fan of second-hand books. *N GOG* has its origins in the cover of a damaged volume on Vincent van Gogh, found in a skip outside a hospital. The letters of the book's cover mysteriously wrap around a central sculpture. Hitesh claims to have always loved the work of Van Gogh, but the phallic suede pillar in the middle of this piece, he explains, is a statement on the male dominance of the art world at the time the Dutch artist was alive. *Blue Box* is made from a pair of basketball boots in which Hitesh played as a child in the streets of north London. Although indicative of a happy childhood, the work also contains family memories brought to England from Africa, as conveyed by the box's interior made from an African jacket and the tribal badge of nails.

Cinthol was Hitesh's first free-standing sculpture, created after spotting a beautiful plinth in a clearance sale. It is probably one of Hitesh's most international creations, using elements found in Australia and India, where he bought the soap that lends the work its title. *Cinthol* holds an extra special memory for Hitesh, as the trip to India proved to be the last time he would visit the country with his father.

CINTHOL
2012, 16 × 10 × 10 cm
Wooden plinth, plastic, thread, electronics, soap, and toy

BLUE BOX
1994, 20 × 16 × 6 cm
Denim canvas, wood, fabric, nails

N GOG
1994, 20 × 16 × 6 cm
Fabric cover, wood, suede, and paint

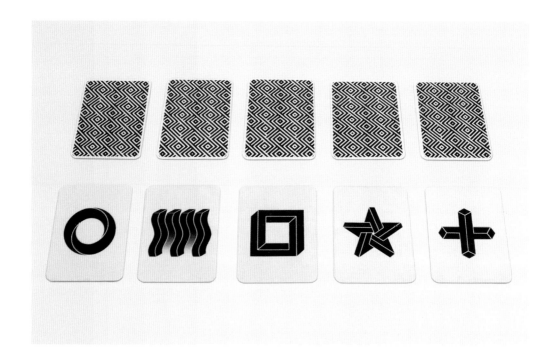

KIT RUSSELL

Kit Russell is an award-winning freelance designer currently based in Dundee, Scotland. His work is notable for its simple yet sophisticated graphic approach, encompassing a variety of different media, including print, packaging, and motion graphics. While experimenting with elements of optical art, his illustrative style focuses on geometry, line, and character informed by a combined use of both traditional and digital design techniques.

ZENER CARDS
2014, a contemporary repackaging of the classic ESP stimulus playing cards, originally used in the 1930s for testing the psychological faculty known as telepathy

LIAM BROMAGE

The work of Liam Bromage, a printmaker by trade, explores the legacy of analogue technology. More specifically, Liam is fascinated by what we are able to say with the use of such "redundant" technological forms.

Interaction is a crucial element in Liam's practice, leading to a generative process. "The work displayed in my shows," he explains, "consists of a typewriter, which uses a carbon paper ribbon embedded with type. I take leftover residue which has been produced by anon as the starting point for works on paper. The typewriter ribbon becomes a kind of matrix and acts as a transfer. I like the versatility that a seemingly simple [object] such as a typewriter ribbon is able to produce. I'm able to take it in many directions. This process is unique to me and is produced through a relief printmaking technique. The prints are paired together to reflect the original matrix, setting up positive and negative images." *Binary Code* was created especially for the *Out of the Box* exhibitions.

BINARY CODE
2012, 16 × 12 × 10 cm
Encased typewriter reel

MICAH LEXIER
SOMETHING I MADE WITH SOME THINGS THAT I FOUND

Micah Lexier is a Toronto-based artist whose activities include making, collecting, and organizing. He is fascinated by measurement, increment, found imagery, and display structures. Micah's projects range in scale from limited-edition multiples to massive public sculptures. He has held more than a hundred solo exhibitions, participated in over two hundred group shows, and has produced a dozen permanent public commissions. His artwork takes many forms, from illuminated light boxes to vitrine installations.

In 2020, Micah created *Several Found Things (Numbers, Letters, Shapes)*, a jigsaw puzzle composed entirely of images of found objects sourced from his archive of teaching tools, games, puzzles, tests, building blocks, stencils, stationery, magic tricks, and a number of utilitarian objects. In creating the puzzle, he selected items featuring numbers, letters, and simple geometric shapes, with a focus on those with multiple or repeated elements. In doing so, he was able to embed a series of small puzzles within the larger puzzle. Made in collaboration with Four Point Puzzles, *Several Found Things* seemed like a natural progression to Micah: an actual, commercially produced puzzle, rather than a work about a puzzle. "I work very intuitively," he says. "I cleared off our dining-room table and just started placing the things I had pre-selected. Every time I walked by the table over a period of a couple of weeks, I would look it over and try to evaluate what was working and what was not. I would move things around, swap things out, remove certain elements, until nothing was bothering me that much. It's important not to drain the spontaneity, so I made an effort to hold myself back from over-working it."

When devising the puzzle, Micah explains, he did not consciously adopt the mindset of a puzzle-maker; rather, the process was almost identical to that behind the creation of one of his vitrine displays. The only difference was that he did not want the puzzle to have a "correct" orientation, which meant he had to think carefully about the way it was laid out. When asked about the items featured in the puzzle, he says: "I don't really have stories behind any of the objects, as they are not related to my past in any way.

Left and opposite
SEVERAL FOUND THINGS
(NUMBERS, LETTERS,
SHAPES)
1,000 piece puzzle
63.5 × 63.5 cm
© *Four Points Puzzle, 2020*

Several Found Things (Numbers, Letters, Shapes)
Micah Lexier

1000

25 x 25 in (63.5 x 63.5 cm) square puzzle

four point puzzles

I purchased most of them from flea markets, antique/thrift stores, or ebay, and in some cases I was given them as gifts. There are two, related objects in the puzzle that are among my favourites. Both are boxes in which something has been printed on the inside of the actual box. The first is a small box that has orange paper on the outside and a thin grid printed on the inside. A detail, which unfortunately you cannot see in the puzzle, is that the printed lines of the grid turn up slightly onto the sides of the box. I just love the simplicity, size, and subtle details of this object. The second is a larger box with a grid of numbers—a multiplication table actually—printed directly on the inside of the box. One of the details I love about this object is that a different typeface has been used on the three-digit numbers. Again, the size and the materiality of the box, combined with the print quality and the typeface choices, are what attract me to this object." Has he ever completed his own puzzle? "Ah, putting me on the spot, eh? Yes, I did complete the puzzle with my partner, but to be honest he did most of it. I'm really glad I did try it out, as I have a much better idea of what kinds of challenges are more pleasurable. And in any subsequent puzzles, I will try to include more of those moments."

Right and pages 292–293
A SELECTION OF OBJECTS FROM MICAH LEXIER'S PERSONAL ARCHIVE

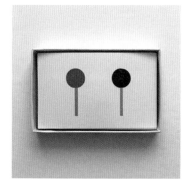

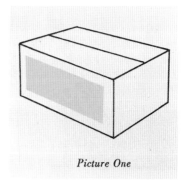

Picture One

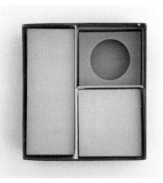

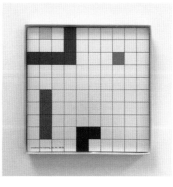

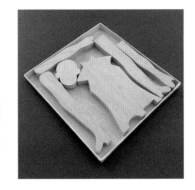
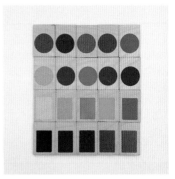
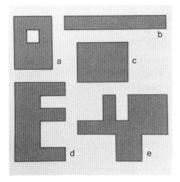

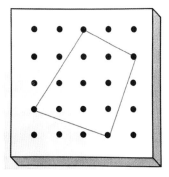

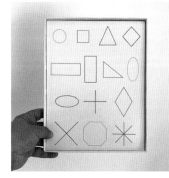

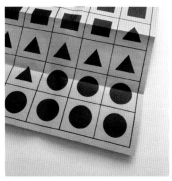

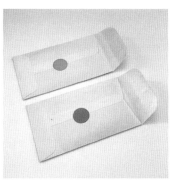

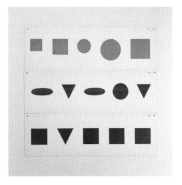

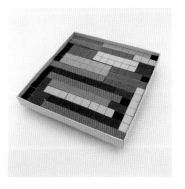

DOCUBYTE

James Ball, aka Docubyte, is a photographer, retoucher, and art director. His mantra is technology is beautiful. "I'm a huge fan of analogue, vintage things," says James. "Dials, switches, and knobs have such a timeless, retro appeal and a kind of innocent charm in the current world of slick, tech gadgetry that I wanted to address this photographically. I began thinking about building a kind of vintage machine myself, but in researching the kind of things I was into, I realized that so many machines existed that looked like what I had in my mind. I didn't need to build anything myself: the analogue machines of my fantasies actually existed in real life."

It was James's interest in documentary photography and his work as a retoucher in the advertising industry that led to "Docubyte"—a coming-together of his passion for historic machines and skill in digital beautification. The series *Guide to Computing* celebrates the world of computers between 1945 and 1990, documenting their evolution. After establishing where he could find a particular machine, James would then arrange a photo shoot. His biggest challenge, given the various locations in which he had to work, was in making the computers look as though they had all been photographed in the same place. Shooting some of them behind glass, such as Alan Turing's Automatic Computing Engine (ACE), proved an additional challenge, but fortunately many of these issues could be resolved in Photoshop. A number of the computers predate modern colour photography; James's visual love letter to the technology of yore thus allows us to see them in an entirely new light.

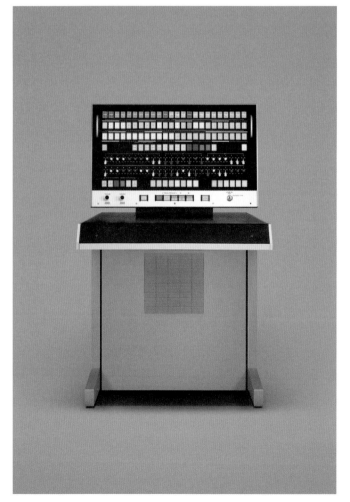

FERRANTI ATLAS, 1964

CRAY 1 SUPERCOMPUTER, 1975

"There was a time not so long ago when computers were not thin, stylish devices you slip into a pocket or wear on your wrist, but enormous, fabulous machines with flashing lights and spinning fans. These behemoths filled rooms and captured imaginations with their promise of the future." *Jenna Garret,* Wired

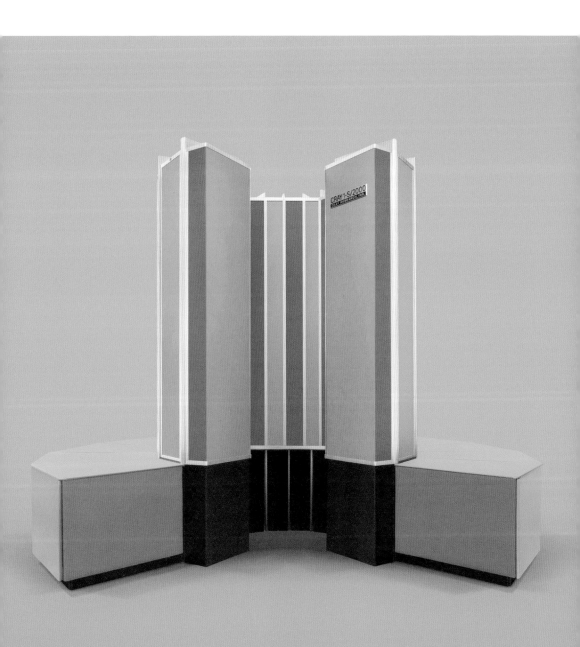

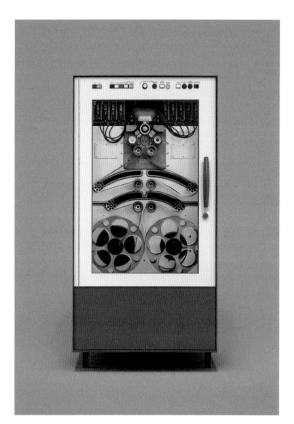

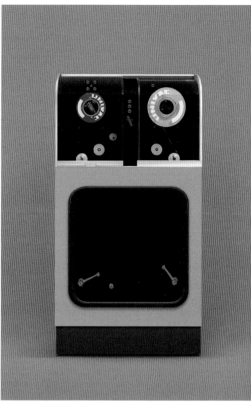

"Never trust a computer you can't throw out of a window."
Steve Wozniak

Clockwise from opposite top left
ELLIOT 803, 1963
UNISERVO, 1951
UNIVAC 9400 SERIES, 1969
TELEFUNKEN RA770, 1966
KENBAK 1, 1970
SCIENTIFIC DATA SYSTEMS (SDS)
920, 1962

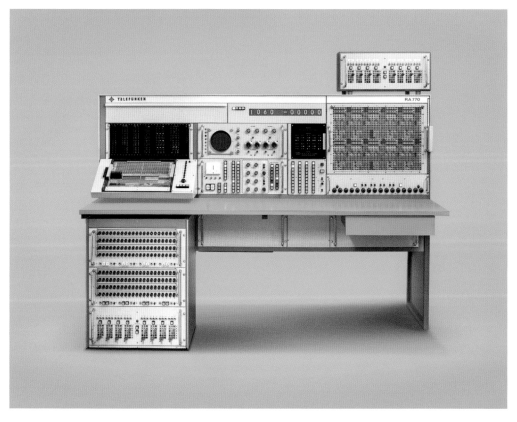

IAN WRIGHT

"Playfulness is important to me; I'm motivated by trying to push my work somewhere new, somewhere else. Really, I'm interested in what could be. I sometimes reach that point by making mistakes and generally misusing technology. I often arrive at solutions by accident. I prefer to let the materials I use influence the outcome."

British artist Ian Wright creates pixel-based portraits using an endless array of different materials. He does not feel nostalgic for any particular era, and is far more interested in what comes next. Ian always wanted to be a commercial artist, getting his big break shortly after college doing weekly portraits for the popular British music newspaper *New Musical Express*. He honed his experimental approach with a groundbreaking, "White Lines"–era portrait of Grandmaster Flash. While trying to tap into something soulful with his subjects, Ian also pushed the boundaries of what you could do with an office copying machine.

During these formative years, Ian worked at London-based NTA Studios with such maverick illustrators as George Hardie and Bush Hollyhead; he also shared a studio with graphic designer, art director, and typographer Neville Brody. An early inspiration is the wall covered with pages ripped from magazines in the 1968 cult film *if…*, which Malcolm McDowell's character uses for target practice. In 2020, informed by his participation in a march in New York City in 2014 protesting the death of Eric Garner, Ian created a portrait of George Floyd, who was killed by a police officer in Minneapolis, Minnesota. Ian used Hama Beads for the portrait—a toy for all ages, as he puts it, with an appealing limited colour palette.

DEE DEE RAMONE
2021, 45 × 60 × 10 cm
Metallic silver and halftone black screen-print on paper
Produced as part of The Mash Up 2, *a collaborative project with photographer Janette Beckman*

THE CLEVER AUSTRALIAN
Portrait of Ahmed Fahour, former head of Australia Post
2013, approx. 1 × 1 metre
Assorted new and used postage stamps
A commission from The Monkeys

REMEMBERING GEORGE FLOYD
2020, 29.5 × 21 × 8 cm
Hama Beads in bespoke frame

MICHAEL JOHANSSON

Swedish artist Michael Johansson re-contextualizes the readymade, freeing mundane objects from their function to produce geometric sculptures and perfectly constructed installations. His real-life Tetris pieces are recognizable yet unique, archaeologies of everyday life compressed into harmonious rectangles or cubes. His sculptures could perhaps be seen as contemporary still lifes, yet they are abstract in the way in which disparate parts have been puzzled together according to shape and colour. Like Marcel Duchamp, Michael takes the mundane out of its usual context, collecting, preserving, and showing.

Objects can often be read like words, making sentences. With his distinctive way of handling objects, presenting them *en masse*, Michael tells a story while building a sculptural design. His use of a consistently monochrome colour scheme bestows his works with form and visual calm, reflecting his obsession with finding doubles of seemingly lone and often useless things. With such projects as *Engine Bought Separately*, he reverse-engineers objects back into model kits, like those that fascinated him as a child. These works comment on our relationship with objects, ironically referencing functionality while at the same time eliminating it. Michael's stand-alone and fill-in sculptures contain and expose simultaneously. They are proof positive of the possibility of thinking inside and outside the box at the same time.

MIRRORCUBE – OCEAN
2020, 30 × 30 × 30 cm
Blue and green ordinary items

ENGINE BOUGHT SEPARATELY –
HUGIN
2007, 49 × 66 × 8 cm
Hair dryer, welded metal frame, spray paint

HARMONY
2021, 18 × 18 × 18 cm
Divisible cube made from red and orange ordinary items

Pages 302–303
TUBE
2013, 36 × 36 × 81 cm
Yellow and orange bags, boxes, and ordinary items

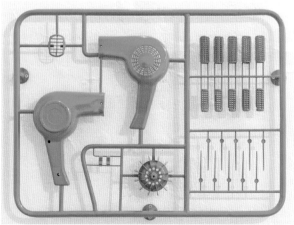

"I am intrigued by irregularities in daily life. Not those that appear when something extraordinary occurs, but those that are created by an exaggerated form of regularity. Colours or patterns from two separate objects or environments concur, like when two people pass each other dressed in the exact same outfit. Or when you are switching channels on your TV and realize that the same actor is playing two different roles on two different channels at the same time." *Michael Johansson*

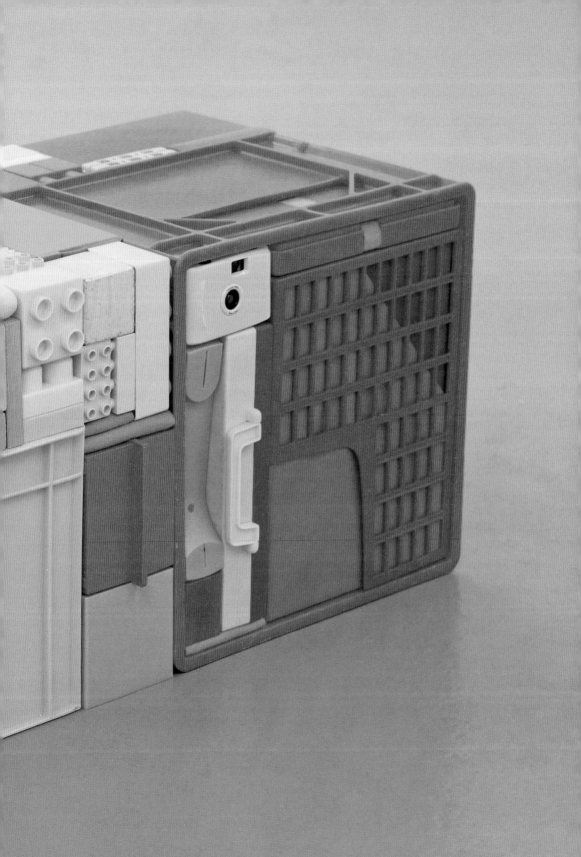

LUKE PENDRELL

Luke Pendrell is a collage artist who is drawn to the edges of things—to science, philosophy, and the occult, to the fictions we construct to make sense of the world. His work has been performed, screened, and exhibited extensively in various institutions and art galleries. He currently works at the Royal College of Art in London.

Discussing his practice, Luke says: "I make paper collages, but I also consider all the work I do, whether writing, film-making, photography, performance, painting, assemblage, sculpture, or installation, to be collage in form. But [perhaps] this scattered practice is better understood not as discrete pieces of work, but as connected fragments of a larger collage. Maybe like Aby Warburg's *Bilderatlas Mnemosyne*, a mad, sprawling, constant reordering of the world's connections and components into new configurations . . .

"Collage is a way of destroying and reordering the world afresh, refusing the given order of things as permanent and irrefutable. It's possible that working in boxes, or glass frames, sets these reorderings in the lost logics of the *Wunderkammer* [cabinet of curiosities], where order and absurdity seem to jostle for position . . . A collage practice is in places curatorial; it gathers together hitherto separate elements. But crucially, collage always moves beyond curation: the fragments are always subsumed by the new roles, constellations, and configurations they are bent to.

"Rather than just a collecting, gathering, or bringing together, in [collage's] irreverent excisions and transposition, a radical transformation takes place, where the sum of the whole is greater than its parts. Collage doesn't just reorder the world, it remakes it. In this scavenging insubordination of the order of things . . . the importance of collage emerges, as it conjures something different from the what-already-is. From this radical difference, collage emerges as something more germinal than parasitic. From amid its disorder and disruption, we sometimes glimpse the emergence of something genuinely new."

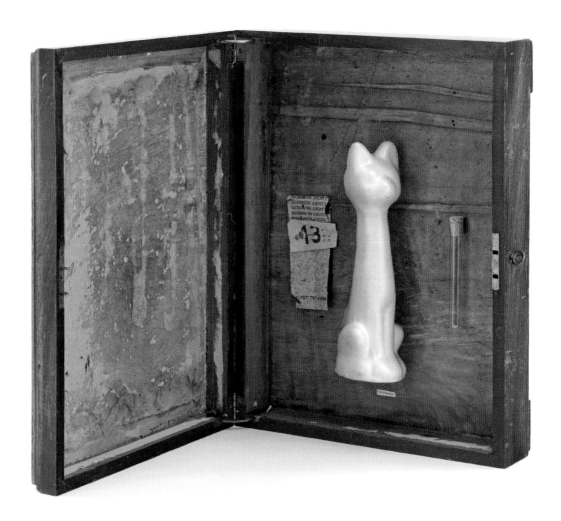

GHOST FACE
2011, 19 × 29 × 7 cm
Wood, tin, and paper

MESSAGES FROM THE DEAD
2014, 40 × 31 × 13 cm
Wood, steel, acetate, cardboard

THE QUANTUM DEMON
2012, 38 × 29 × 9 cm
Wood, ceramic, test tube, and paper

THE PROPHECIES OF CAZOTTE
2012, 29 × 29 × 5 cm
Oil on board, acetate

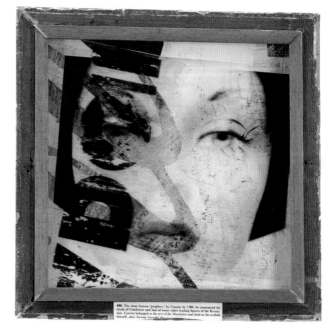

DONALD RODNEY

Born in Birmingham, England, in 1961, Donald Gladstone Rodney was a leading figure in the UK's BLK Art Group of the 1980s and became known as "one of the most innovative and versatile artists of his generation." In his work, Rodney appropriated images from the media, art, and popular culture to explore issues of racial identity. He was a multifaceted artist, working in a range of mediums—from painting, installation, and photography to robotics, film, and computers—yet often defied simple categorization, in either theme or approach.

Having been diagnosed with sickle cell anaemia at a young age, Donald chose to incorporate this illness into his work, using it to explore black emasculation, racial stereotyping, and wider sociopolitical concerns in contemporary society. Donald finally succumbed to the disease in March 1998, aged just thirty-six.

Two of Donald's works are shown here with the kind assistance of Iniva (Institute of International Visual Arts). Challenging our conceptions of cultural, physical, and social identity, *Mexico Olympics* and *John Barnes* are photographic images displayed on rudimentary light boxes. The former depicts two black athletes raising their fists in the Black Power salute at the 1968 Olympics. The latter shows the ex-Liverpool and England footballer kicking away a banana that had been thrown at him from the crowd. These are iconic images of defiance and determination at a time when racism was rife in the media and black sportsmen were fighting to be seen as equals. More than thirty years after these works were made, racism remains a toxic disease that must be overcome.

Above left
MEXICO OLYMPICS
1991, 180 × 107 × 18 cm
Light box,
fluorescent tube
Collection of the Estate
of Donald Rodney

Above right
JOHN BARNES
1991, 180 × 107 × 18 cm
Light box,
fluorescent tube
Collection of the Estate
of Donald Rodney

RACHEL SMITH

Prompted by the startling fact that the British supermarket chain Tesco currently stocks 141 types of toothpaste, Rachel Smith's installation *Order, Disorder and (the Anxiety of) Choice* is a pensive testimonial to the contemporary fascination with choice. At once both an opportunity and a necessity, choosing is increasingly synonymous with responsibility, resulting in success, failure, or, worse yet, stagnant mediocrity. What to eat, how to look, where to live, when and how to start a family, how to spend one's free time and money, how to vote, "no fluoride," "outstanding whitening," "with spicy fresh cooling crystals"—one should at all times strive to make the "right" decision.

This imperative to choose and choose well results in a continual process of calculative ordering: price, quality, intuition, simplicity, appearance, sustainability, past experience, distance, calorie content. For many, this process of arduously pursuing the perfect choice can collapse into a chaotic amalgamation of disorderly thoughts, highlighting the delicate balance between the freedom to choose and the tyranny of choosing. Paired with the excessive and overwhelming abundance of choices that can, could, or should be made at every step and scale, this neurotic obsession with the endlessly (re)calculable "right" decision can have a debilitating effect on mental well-being, resulting in dissatisfaction, anxiety, and an overall malaise.

Rachel is an artist and creative technologist currently based at the Pervasive Media Studio in Bristol, England, where she also lives. Often making use of such diverse media as DIY electronics, hacking, found objects, software, and paint, her work takes a critical look at the technologies that affect us on an everyday level but are wrapped in a cloak of complexity. She is particularly interested in interactivity, the relationship and collaboration between humans and non-humans.

ORDER, DISORDER AND (THE ANXIETY OF) CHOICE
2014, installation of miscellaneous toothpastes

FRANK KUNERT
STAIRWAYS TO HEAVEN

"Buildings say something about people. They are the expression of our culture, our past, our present, and our future."
Elizabeth Clarke, "Wunderland"

Based in his native Germany, Frank Kunert is a photographer and model-maker. He started taking photographs as a teenager, showing a particular interest in landscape photography. After training as a photographer, he nurtured a love for studio work, which remains his focus today, designing and photographing his fastidious micro-worlds.

At first glance, Frank's miniature scenes resemble mundane, everyday domestic settings, with the same beige colour palette and concrete walls that are common across the globe. On closer inspection, however, his work reveals itself to be a series of surreal scenarios, a fantastical journey in which humdrum objects are transformed and merged into unusual architectural scenes that explore the absurdity of life.

Frank's bizarre wonderlands are reflections not only of our fears and needs but also of our desires. They bring home the many ludicrous aspects of the everyday: the grotesque attempts to organize our lives, the disappearance of old traditions, the way we deal with one another and with our history. His contemplative constructions are nevertheless more life-affirming and funny than incriminating. The inner worlds of our homes are invariably reflections of the zeitgeist and represent much of what goes on both inside and around us.

Frank's constructions can take weeks or months to complete. He then photographs them using a digital camera with a "tilt-shift" lens. Among other things, they demonstrate his great skill in using everyday objects to inspire viewers to consider how *they* might use old collectibles or discarded items for whole new purposes. Like that of other artists, Frank's practice has been shaped by the Covid-19 pandemic, and many of his designs reflect the strictures that we have all had to face. Taking an old wooden table, for example, he divided it into individual booths for insatiable diners.

DAYDREAM

CLIMBING HOLIDAYS

Slowness is key to Frank's practice, made possible by his craftsmanship and patience in building these miniature worlds with precise studio lighting. The preparation has a devotional quality, in which layer upon layer of paint is meticulously applied to the model. Construction errors are always welcome; as in real life, paint runs, colour fades, and plaster falls off the wall. Improvisation is as much a part of Frank's work as well-planned precision. Minuscule inventiveness is also constant. Several layers of lovingly applied paint, for example, might turn the lid of a bottle of household cleaner into a rubbish bin, salt into snow, or wads of cotton into clouds or steam; likewise, the dispenser from a bottle of washing-up liquid is wondrously transformed into an inlet pipe, and a doily into a curtain.

Before Frank can create one of his worlds, lightweight foam boards are cut. Things are then glued, painted, and varnished; floors are laid, windows installed; the odd piece of furniture or musical instrument is made; curtains get hung; tiles are laid, rooms furnished, roofs shingled; trees are planted; backgrounds and walls are painted. At times, the process seems to blur the boundary between photography and painting. Frank's award-winning creations are regularly exhibited in Germany and abroad and have been published extensively. Small worlds of tragedy and comedy, they are an unconventional declaration of love to the innumerable stories—our stories—that make up everyday life.

Clockwise from top right
HEAVEN'S GATE
THE LAST JOURNEY
ETERNAL LOVE

Pages 312–313
ROOM WITH A VIEW (and artist)

311

ROSIE ROOPE

As a young illustrator, Rosie Roope discovered that she liked working at events, interacting with people and working under pressure. In 2011, in response to a request to create something for the "Big Draw" event in her friend's shop, she built a "portrait booth" out of cardboard, drawing people in three minutes while hiding in a box. This then turned into the *Photo Booth* project. Today, the booth can be hired for such events as weddings and music festivals—although you might encounter a sign announcing that Rosie has gone to see her favourite band. Pictured here is the booth at the End of the Road festival in Dorset's Larmer Tree Gardens.

A sign attached to the booth promises "Real Likeness, 30% accuracy, High-Def, 4D, Dolby." "I mainly do weddings these days," says Rosie, explaining that she gives the portraits of attending guests away for free. "It really makes me happy. I love the fact that I can do this as a job, get to make people laugh, draw all day, and eat a ton of amazing cake."

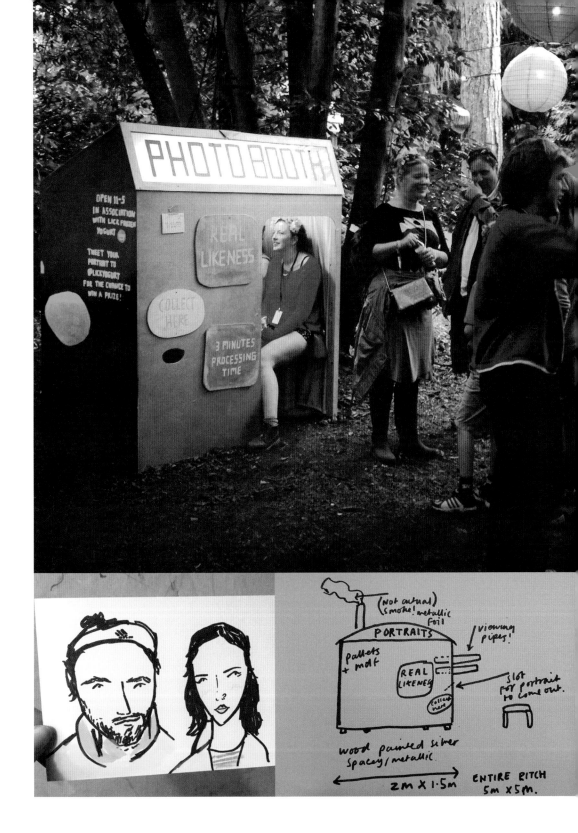

  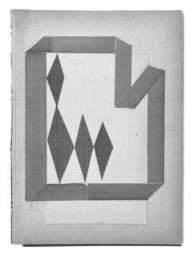

LAURI HOPKINS

"I work in groups. In fact, in groups of groups. Paintings affect collages, discarded materials are reconfigured and masquerade as paintings. Everything feeds back into everything else. Works are named after songs, painters, relatives, buildings—stuff of the human world mostly."

Underpinning everything that Lauri Hopkins makes is an understanding of colour and a fascination with the way we see everyday objects. Whether painting on top of found objects, or simply re-configuring them, her process is purely intuitive and unfolding. "I try to work in an open way," she explains, "and intend for the works themselves to open out into countless connections. I hope that there is a sense of everythingness about them." Lauri's inspirations include mid-century architecture and design, the history of abstract art, and objects that have become defunct and fallen out of use.

Created from a genuine and responsive place, bodies of work become celebratory visual diaries. Lauri has spent years amassing a collection of found materials, including book covers, sweet wrappers, and cardboard. These materials form a starting point; from there, idiosyncratic compositions build, shed, and build again. The process is never linear, instead taking the form of an unfolding, intuitive puzzle. A box frame provides the ideal vehicle for conveying the textures and exquisite bricolage quality of Lauri's work. During the Covid-19 pandemic, her art was in much demand, with one smitten buyer purchasing an entire wall of works. One wonders if they will recreate the original arrangement in a specially built cabinet.

SELECTED WORKS
2020–2021

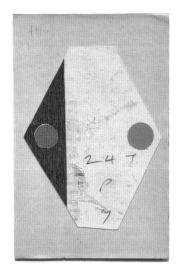

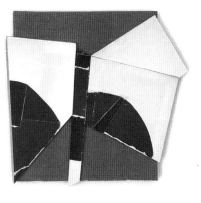

GRAHAM CARTER

In addition to being a successful commercial illustrator and an award-nominated writer of children's books, Graham Carter is one of the UK's most prolific and collected printmakers. His work brings together a myriad of creatures and characters, fantastical landscapes, and comical fan art, all presented in a number of themes and styles. As a master printmaker, Graham creates all his artworks himself, experimenting with various printmaking techniques, painting, hand-drawing, and three-dimensional modelling. Foils, flocks, and enamels play a large part in bringing Graham's characters to life, creating incredible depth and detail.

The three-dimensional work was first made for a solo exhibition entitled *Me, Marionette*. Inspired by the story of Pinocchio and the birth of his first child, Graham began contemplating his son's future and the world in which he will grow up, the influences surrounding him and the person he might become. "I liked the idea that there might be alternative versions of Pinocchio out there," explains Graham, "and that each has a specific role in life and a destiny to fulfil. I've put myself in the role of Geppetto in creating these marionettes and tried to inject elements of my own personality and interests in their make-up."

THE WARRIOR (detail)
2012, 68 × 44 × 7 cm
Laser-cut/etched painted plywood,
silk-screened details

THE ASTRONAUT
2012, 66 × 40 × 7 cm
Laser-cut/etched painted plywood and
Perspex, silk-screened details

NEARLY PINOCCHIO
2012, 66 × 44 × 7 cm
Silk-screened and painted laser-cut/
etched plywood

Discussing the making of his works, Graham says: "I fell in love with the process of planning, laser-cutting, and assembling my new toy creations. Early on in the process I would sometimes negate the fact that in real life layers don't float in mid-air as they do on the computer, and need a backing to stick to. Half the fun is trying to hone the process and problem-solve through trial and error. I now plan them fairly meticulously on Photoshop beforehand, to get an idea where pieces will fit during the layering. I love breaking away from the rigidness of computer design to bring these elements into the physical world. The most daunting stage is to lay out all the 'jigsaw'-type components and do a 'dummy' fit. Then I individually paint and screen-print designs onto them, with a bit of roughing up by sanding to age them. Then I may repaint areas and re-sand, finished off with glue or nuts and bolts to hold them together, taking some of the weight once attached to a backing board. This part tends to add a little more character, creating the retro aesthetic that appeals to me so much. I draw a lot of inspiration from trips to flea markets, where you might see old penny arcade machines or forgotten treasures. Basically anything with clunky clockwork technology."

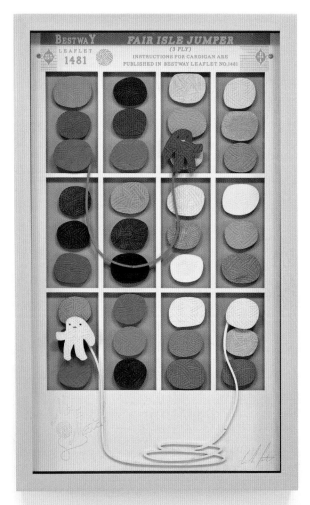

Left (detail top)
MIX 'N' MATCH
2013, 64 × 40 × 7 cm
Silk-screened and painted laser-cut/ etched plywood

Opposite
THE DIRECTOR
2012, 54 × 33 × 7 cm
Silk-screened and painted laser-cut/ etched plywood

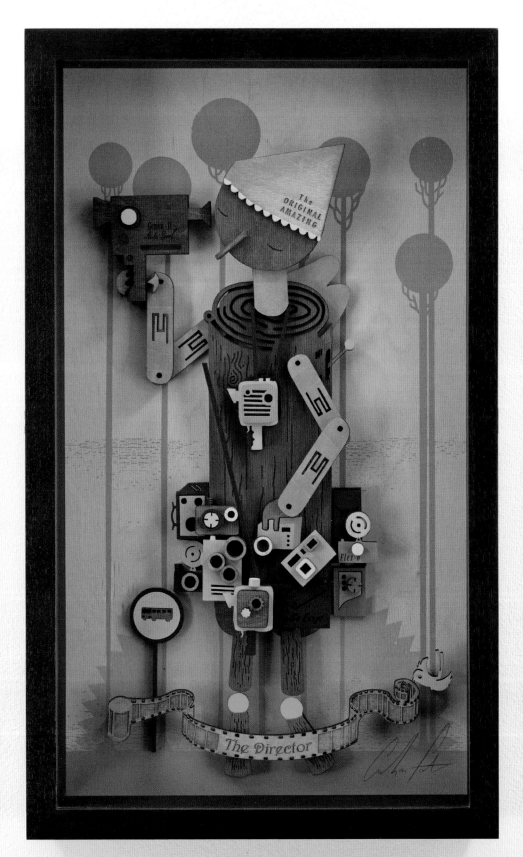

KATE ILES

"I'm quite nostalgic for the past. I could do without a phone; I don't really like the internet; if it all went down I'd be quite happy! My work tends to be from a certain era, and often has that wartime feel to it. I know it wasn't a gentler time at all, but certain elements were a lot nicer. It's also about needing to preserve stuff. Whole lives are left in junk shops or house clearances and I just can't bear to leave them there. I find that tragic. I'm really fascinated with the element of chance; I like how some things have survived and resurfaced and the journey they take. And most important is the human connection with everyday items—old tins, keys, whatever."

Based in Hastings, East Sussex, Kate Iles enjoys nothing more than finding dusty old boxes in junk shops full of black-and-white photographs, momentary faces frozen in time. She revives the forgotten lives of the photographs' subjects as illuminated vignettes with a shrine-like quality. Framing these "snapshots" in relief is a totally instinctive process, with ideas coming from such sources as the photos themselves or chit-chat overheard on the high street or in her favourite Hastings shop, the legendary Roberts Rummage.

Kate's latest project involves some old photos and letters she found in two suitcases bought at auction. The correspondence is between a mother, her daughter, and her son. The daughter's letters came first from a privileged boarding school, then from what appears to be an institution, and finally from a prison, while the mother travelled around the world never writing back. As Kate says, we will never know the answers; instead, it is all about the gaps in the narrative.

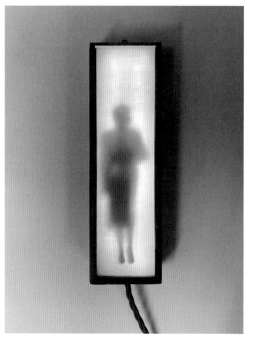

JAUNTY GUY
2021, 26 × 19 × 6 cm
Unframed mixed-media collage

PENELOPE (MYSTERY LADY)
2022, 22 × 7 × 6 cm
Mixed-media assemblage, electronics

BILLIE'S GRANNY
2017, 23 × 22 × 20 cm
Vintage photo, mixed media, electronics

SEMOR & CO.

Richard Coldicott, aka Semor, grew up in Birmingham, England, a city interwoven with the detritus of industrial collapse. He has always been fascinated by the look and feel of abandoned spaces, once valued and thriving. Even before the convenience of a smartphone, Richard was never without a camera, documenting at random. Typography and graphic elements often took precedence, but pattern, composition, surface, and patina did not go unnoticed.

Richard's works on wood are essentially hand-painted recreations of the things he finds interesting in the street. The use of wood, he says, feels right. In most cases it is true to the source material, plus the "weathering" he adds feels almost believable. Some pieces remain abstract, while others fuse together multiple elements to form their own social narrative. These assortments are collections, revisited diary pages, fragments of places once visited, all pulled together and thrown into the box.

The name "Semor" is a tag from Richard's spray-paint roots. "Semor & Co." is still a pseudonym of sorts, but less graffiti-writer and more fictional sign-painter of yore, long since gone out of business. Having trained as a hand-drawn/stop-motion animator, Richard currently works in moving image, primarily using video (or sometimes film, budgets permitting). He found the suitcase that makes up *Untitled* in the street; it was, he says, simply too nice to leave behind. "The labels and marks are just beautiful. I added a few of my own, most obviously the lettering, albeit as respectfully as I felt possible."

BELLY UP (top) & SPENT (centre)
2010, 40 × 40 × 6 cm
Paint on wooden panels

UNTITLED
2012, 44 × 58 × 14 cm
Printed label and paint on found suitcase

MARK THURGOOD

Mark Thurgood is all about interiors, specializing in individual pieces of functional furniture, from tables to sideboards. He is drawn to surprising, fascinating combinations of modern and industrial design—what he calls "the breaking of the rules." Mark avidly collects what many of us would assume is junk, which he then turns into artworks for sale, or little "landscape moments throughout the house."

It is rare to see Mark without his trademark flat cap and canvas smock jacket, a sharpened pencil at the ready, tucked into his top pocket. Mark relishes problem-solving with limited resources. His "tennis settee," made of striking tennis balls, achieved national recognition. The project began after discovering a sofa dumped on the street; all the tennis balls were donated by Telford Park Lawn Tennis Club in Streatham, south London. In Mark's hands, materials never go to waste, including in his ongoing *Tiny Houses* series, which consists of wooden, house-like building blocks whittled from offcuts to be displayed ornately.

Mark thanks his father for encouraging him as a boy to use his workbench and tools in the garden shed. This early experience set Mark up for a lifetime of making three-dimensional work, from go-carts to oak tables. *Hand Drawn Is Best* was inspired by a vintage child's desk. What appears quite dull and sombre, with haunting memories of school work, is transformed in an instant when you lift the lid to reveal an explosion of colour. A clarion call to creatives young and old!

HAND DRAWN
IS BEST
2014, 40 × 30 × 40 cm
Vintage desk,
chalk, Andy Smith
illustration, pencil

Head & Shoulders was inspired by David Beckham's career-defining performance against Greece in the decisive game of England's qualifying campaign for the 2002 World Cup. During the course of the game, Beckham gave a true captain's performance. At times, it seemed as though he was single-handedly carrying his weary team-mates through the game, running an extraordinary 16.1 kilometres in the process. In a moment of pure sporting melodrama, he clinched victory for England with a trademark free kick in the final moments.

The language of football is littered with hackneyed phrases. However, the physical superiority of the central figure in *Head & Shoulders* brings actuality to an old idiom much beloved of commentators on the national game. It takes as its basis a row of table footballers, one of whom is significantly taller than his fellow players. The piece also gives a knowing wink to the affectionate nickname that the tabloid press bestowed on the nation's favourite footballer: at the feet of the totemic figure sits a golden ball.

HEAD & SHOULDERS
2010, 15 × 140 × 10 cm
Solid aluminium, stainless steel,
pewter, lead, brass, and gold leaf

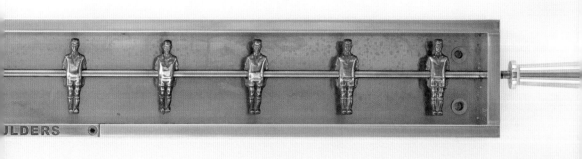

"I own a 1960s wooden chalet on the north Cornwall shore looking across to St Ives. Every year, in February/March, it requires maintenance and painting. On my beach walks I fell into the habit of picking up various plastics trapped in the rocks. I love the white dusty patina [plastic] emits as it starts to break down in respect to the elements. On one occasion I noticed an old friend from school and asked him what he was doing these days. He replied, "Oh, I'm stuck in a dull management job in Basingstoke. What are you doing now?" I proudly answered, "Collecting yellow," and felt like a king." *Mark Thurgood*

COLLECTING
YELLOW
2012, 60 × 120 × 20 cm
Nearly all plastic
waste found on one
Cornish beach over
ten years

Exhibition posters by Tom Buchanan, with the exception of "Boxes" (bottom right) by Paul Burgess

The author at No Format Gallery, Second Floor Studios & Arts (SFSA), London SE18

ACKNOWLEDGEMENTS

I would like to thank all the members of the box gang, without whose blind faith this book would not have been possible. And, of course, Laura my love, and Scruffie and Mike; my folks!

POLICE WHISTLE WITH EYES
by Nancy Fouts
2011, 5 × 3 × 2 cm
Antique police whistle, glass eye

In no particular order, a very special thank you to Matthew Wood, Stephen Baycroft, Nichole Herbert Wood, Second Floor Studios & Arts, Peter Mallet, Catherine Phelps, Robert Lee, Mark Fletcher, Damian Jaques, Max Benham, Sophie Jegado, Philip Oakley, Jamie Hawkins, Paul Stolper, Lucie Bergeron-Johnson, Steve Lowe/Sophie Polyviou and L-13 Light Industrial Workshop, Alexandra Noble, Mischa Eligoloff, Roger Thorp, Keren Luchtenstein, Present & Correct, Emy Gray and BRIXI, England & Co., Katarina Bergström and Galleri GKM, the Yrjö Edelmann Estate, Julian Rothenstein, Nick Appleton, 50 Watts, all the "Sewn Antidote" participants, Maria Kilcoyne, Olivia Swift, Simina Neagu, Amrita Dhallu, INIVA, the Estate of Donald Rodney, Sue Smallwood, Jonathan Safran Foer, Rhian Harris, the V&A Museum of Childhood, Alessandro Lorenzetti, Layla Hyun and the Pontone Gallery, Arran Hodgson, Scarlett Mosnier, Tiny Monuments, Artsadmin, Andreina Cordani, Holly Peel and the Wellcome Collection, soundtracks by Helen Murphy, Four Points Puzzles, Olivia Turner, the Royal Scottish Academy of Art, Kristen N. Quarles, the Smithsonian Institution and the staff of the storage collections, Tony Sephton, OSR Projects, Sue Jackson and Cabaret Mechanical Theatre, Carol Butler, Idané Burger and the SMAC Gallery, the Living Arts, Marina Mantoan and Galeria Luisa Strina, Rodrigo Moura, Chronicle Books, Jo and James Woodall, Tim Adams, Dave Swindells, Deborah Curtis and Gavin Turk, Laurent Chéhère, Alexandra Granditsch, Flowers Gallery, Gerald Zaltman, Jack White and Third Man Records, Gina Cross, Ryan Stanier and the Other Art Fair, Laura Devine, Fiona Foster and Heiner Schuff, Nat Foreman, Simon Hollingsworth, Alex Binnie, Lucy Middleton-Carlyle, Charles Troy, Adam Lucy, Ink Spot Press.

PICTURE CREDITS

All photography by Peter Mallet unless otherwise stated in the book or below.

t = top
b = bottom
c = centre
l = left
r = right

WATER

24, 25 Ben Young; 26, 27 David Cass; 30, 31 Julie Speed; 32, 33 SMAC Gallery, © Cyrus Kabiru; 42, 43 Katharine Morling; 44, 45 Rabban; 47 Sean Madden; 58t Anya Beaumont; 60–61 Rob Wass; 62 Justin Piperger; 63 Tom Buchanan; 65b Bob Marshall; 66b Stuart Milne; 69b Julia Maddison; 70–72 Mohamad Hafez; 73 Alex Olevitch, 74–75 Rodney Nelson; 78–79 Ruth Ward; 80–83 Peter Bennetts; 85 Maria Rivans

EARTH

91–95 Deepti Nair and Harikrishnan Paniker; 98, 99 Chris Jenkins; 100, 101 Matthew Tugwell; 102 Jack and Jane Photography; 104t, 106b Glenn Anderson; 104b, 107 Tom Buchanan; 106 *Sun Ra* by Jolyon Holroyd; 108–113 Julie Liger-Belair; 120, 121 Linda Hubbard; 122l London Media; 122t, 123 Tom Brannigan; 125 Michael Vaughan; 126, 128, 130–131 Frank Jennings; 134, 135 Steffen Dam & The Heller Gallery; 136–137 Joanna Bird Gallery; 138t Emma Lloyd; 152 John Dilnot; 154b Graham Woodall; 156, 157 Mark Oliver; 158t Paul Zac; 158b Jonathan Beer; 159 Helen Musselwhite; 162b Tony Eastman

FIRE

165–168 D*Face Studio; 170, 171 Wayne Chisnall; 172, 173 Rosie Mayell; 180–183 Sylvie Giai-Miniet; 184–189 Nancy Fouts; 190, 191 Tom Buchanan; 192, 193 Achim Kukulies; 194–195 Wolfgang Stiller; 196, 197 Keelertornero; 198, 199 Martin O'Neill; 202b, 203 Pontone Gallery; 202t, 204–205 Kim Bumsu; 206–211 Gil Ortiz; 214, 216, 217 Tom Buchanan; 215 Rabban; 218–221 Andrew Shallcross; 222, 223 Emre Uzer; 224b Clare Winnan; 228 Jimmy Cauty; 230 L-13 Light Industrial Workshop; 231t Sam Millen; 231c Bruce Trainer; 232–233 Thomas Mayer; 234b, 235t Edouard Fraipont; 235b, 236–237 Marcelo Arruda; 238–241 Paolo Giardi; 242, 243 Alexander Korzer Robinson; 248b Bryan Benge

AIR

252–255 Daniel Agdag; 256, 257 Benjamin Shine; 258, 259 Love Hultén; 260, 261 John Morgan; 262, 263 Mark Copeland; 266 Rabban; 270t Thomas Jervis; 274t Tom Buchanan; 278, 279 Galleri GKM; 282, 283 Tim Can; 286 Kit Russell; 288, 289 Finn O'Hara; 290–293 Micah Lexier; 294–297 James Ball; 298t Janette Beckman; 298b Ryan Dixon; 299 Tom Buchanan; 300–303 Michael Johansson; 306 George Torode; 307t Rachel Smith; 307b Tom Buchanan; 314, 315b Rosie Roope; 315t Jay Morton; 316, 317 Lauri Hopkins, 322 Kate Iles; 324b Richard Coldicott

INDEX

This book is dedicated to the memory of Nancy Fouts,
Graham Woodall, Yrlö Edelmann, Donald Rodney,
Richard Johnson, and Francesca Lowe.

Tom Buchanan is an artist, curator, collector,
and landscape gardener. This is his first book.

Sarah Lea is a curator at the Royal Academy of Arts,
London. She curated *Joseph Cornell: Wanderlust* in 2015.

HAVE A NICE DAY
by Peter Quinnell
2012, 14 × 10 × 8 cm
Mixed-media assemblage